MW01173589

This book soothed my sou~ ~~ ~~~~~~ ~ ~
faithfulness and compassion of God to His people.

Kari Lee, M.A.
English Faculty, Pueblo Community College

Many want to return to the Book of Acts and the first-century church. Not me! Why? Every miracle, and so much more, recorded in the twenty-eight chapters of Acts in about thirty years of church history, is happening daily with the present-day church. Miracles of supply, healing, deliverance, and salvation abound as waves of God's grace and power flood the earth. Barbara Westberg and her many contributors confirm what I've known all along. Look what God is doing today, not yesterday, and not hundreds of years ago. Claim your miracle today. Barbara and friends will increase your faith!

Jim Poitras
Director of Education/Short-Term Missions
Global Missions, UPCI

Stories of the Supernatural, 70 Present-Day Miracles is just what my soul needed to end the uncertain, roller coaster year of 2020. The same God who parted seas and raised the dead when He walked on this earth, is the same God who heals our loved ones, rescues the drug-addicted teenager, provides jobs for desperate fathers, and so much more.

Barbara Westberg has given us a faith-building treasure in this beautiful compilation of stories. I am excited to share it with my children. I cannot wait to watch their eyes and expressions when we hear about ordinary people receiving extraordinary miracles. The world and its cynicism have a way of chipping away at our ability to believe the supernatural. However, Barbara's book is going to be a valuable tool in helping us reinforce His Word and combat the notion that miracles are a thing of the past. Is there anything my God cannot do?

Pebble Wisdom
Pastor's wife, mother of three
B.A. elementary education, UPCI minister

Stories of the Supernatural

70 Present-Day Miracles

Stories of the Supernatural

70 Present-Day Miracles

A chronicle of miracles

as seen and heard by faithful witnesses

recorded so the generation to come will know

Barbara Westberg

Edited by Kari Lee

Cover designed by Jennifer Short

Stories of the Supernatural
70 Present-Day Miracles

© Barbara Westberg, December 2020

Published in the United States

ISBN: 9798588574679
Imprint: Independently published

Cover by Jennifer Short

DEDICATED TO

Orin Wayne
Huntley Mitchell
Hollyn Irena
and their generation

"We will not hide *them* from their children, shewing to the generation to come the praises of the LORD, and his strength, and his wonderful works that he hath done. That the generation to come might know *them, even* the children *which* should be born; *who* should arise and declare *them* to their children" (Psalm 78:5-6).

CONTENTS

Acknowledgements

To my in-house editor and patient encourager, Francis, the man who has stood by my side for decades, never complaining about the hours (days) I spent at the computer lost in the world of writing while he scrounged in the refrigerator, searching for leftovers not green with mold.

To my daughter Lori and son-in-law Paul who pulled and pushed and pressed me to finish this work I had begun. Plagued is too strong a word, but they would not let me quit.

To the fifty-three witnesses who took time to share their personal miracles. Their names are listed with their stories.

To Kari Lee, whose professional skills make me look like a better writer than I am.

To Jennifer Short, designer extra-ordinaire, whom Francis and I proudly claim as our "other granddaughter."

And, finally, to the God of miracles Who delights in showing Himself strong on behalf of His children.

Introduction

The sixty-eighth miracle in this book should be the first one, but that would upend the alphabetical order, a big no-no to my analytical mind.

A few years ago, my friend Marilyn Chennault told me the story of "The Missionary and the Hen." Her close friend Kathryn Hendrix, a missionary to China in the 1940s, shared it with her. I remember Missionary Hendrix coming to the small country church my family attended when I was a child. She taught the congregation a song in Chinese (probably Mandarin), that I remember to this day; although I doubt anyone fluent in that language would recognize it. Would the tune "Bringing in the Sheaves" help with the interpretation? Perhaps. My friend and the missionary have since moved to Glory taking their memories with them.

While writing Kathryn Hendrix's miracle for a children's lesson, I wondered, "How many more miracles are in danger of being lost as my generation finishes their earthly journey?"

To preserve a few of these mighty works of God, I sent a plea to my friends, "Tell me your family's miracle, the one that is not widely known, the miracle you want your children and grandchildren to hear and remember."

This book is the result.

As you read these wonder-full stories may you, like me, pause to say, "Wow! Unbelievable." Isn't that what a miracle is . . . an unbelievable act of God, which we must believe because it is true? And may you sing along with me, "There is nothing, no nothing, that my God can't do."

Barbara Westberg

MIRACLES OF DELIVERANCE

A Knock at the Door

As told by Cesar Velez

Knock! Knock! *What was that?* Nine-year-old Cesar jerked awake and peered into the darkness. He could not see a thing, but he heard someone knocking at the apartment door. Fear froze him.

Knock! Knock! *Who was knocking in the middle of the night? Why weren't his parents checking? Was it the police . . . again?* Curiosity overcame fear. The little boy shoved back the blanket and swung his feet onto the cold tile floor. Silently, he crept down the dark hall.

Light outlined the living room door frame. *Were the police outside shining a search light on the door?* Carefully, Cesar lifted the slats on the blind covering the window beside the door. Peeping out he saw a man dressed in brilliant white. The light radiating from him blinded Cesar. He could not make out any facial features, but he knew when the man turned and looked deep into his soul. A presence like he had never felt before flooded the room.

Cesar fell to the floor, weeping. For four or five hours the little boy lay there, sobbing out fear, anger, and hurt. His tears released a longing that his nine-year-old mind could not vocalize, as an indescribable presence surrounded him. As Friday's dawn awoke, the little boy blew his nose and crept back to bed. His parents and siblings had slept through the long night.

Fast forward ten years. It was late evening in a park in Alamogordo, New Mexico. Tension was tight. The air cracked with profanities. The drug deal had gone down. A gun was pointed at Cesar's head.

Click! Click! Nothing. The gun malfunctioned.

"Let's get out of here!" Cesar shouted to his druggie buddy.

Soaked with sweat and gasping for breath, he burst into his family's apartment in the projects. He collapsed on the mangy sofa.

His heart was still hammering against his chest wall when his bubbling sisters breezed into the apartment. "Why, Cesar, what's wrong with you?"

He sat up and hid his face in his hands, trying to calm his trembling. He did not answer.

The girls' countenances sobered. "Cesar, we prayed for you tonight at church."

An alarm sounded in his brain. *That's why the gun didn't go off.* A wake-up call. It was time to get right with God. He knew where to go. He remembered hearing people worshipping as he dealt drugs in the alley behind the church. It was the church his sisters attended.

When Cesar walked into Peace Tabernacle, he felt something that he had not felt for ten years. It was the same presence that filled the room that night when he was nine years old. Love drew him. Love accepted him as he was—multiple piercings, shaved head, baggy clothes, chains clanking (both physically and spiritually). Love changed him.

A few months later Cesar was baptized in Jesus' name. As he came out of the water, Jesus spoke to him, "Before I knocked, but you did not open the door. This time you opened the door, and I have entered."

At this writing Cesar Velez celebrates twenty years drug-free. He has a beautiful family, a profitable occupation, and a ministry reaching others who are responding to the knock at their heart's door.

"Behold, I stand at the door, and knock: if any man hear my voice, and open the door, I will come in to him, and will sup with him, and he with me" (Revelation 3:20).

A Miracle of Mercy

By Deanna Barnes

The C word smacked my sister Leah in July. On my way to the hospital, I remembered how our mother had taught us to love the Lord. When divorce shattered our family, my sister's struggle with learning disabilities had intensified. Without the support she needed, she had run away at seventeen, searching for love.

In the chilly hospital, fear roared in my head. Rough voices echoed from Room 210. "Leah, what's going on? Can't you get a grip? What are you watching anyway? Your dumb soaps, I suppose?"

I peeked around the curtain; she reached for me. Tears flowed.

After Leah's friends left, a doctor entered the room. "Good evening. I'm Dr. Kelly."

Leah sat up. "What did you see on the X-ray?"

"Leah, please, let me take some time—"

"I have been waiting since noon. I'm starving. When can I eat?"

"In a few minutes," he said as he reached for her hand. "I consulted with Dr. Ortiz. We have decided not to operate."

"So . . . this is good news?"

"Leah, surgery will make you feel worse. The cancer has invaded your liver."

She took a deep breath. "What about chemo?"

"You'll need to talk to an oncologist. You may decide chemotherapy will make your remaining days miserable."

Leah turned her head to the wall.

A crushing compression hit my chest. "Remaining days? . . . How much time do you think she has?"

"Only God knows. Every person is different. I have been surprised many times." The doctor turned to Leah. "All of us are dying. The end will come for each of us. In one way you are fortunate because you have time to prepare."

Leah did not speak.

"Would you like me to pray with you, Leah?"

Dr. Kelly's prayer settled over me like a warm blanket. After Leah slept, I opened my Bible. I'd never noticed Micah 7:18 in such detail. "God delights in mercy." Peace tiptoed into the room.

Weeks passed. My sister's sunken eyes asked questions I could not answer. Yet, we discovered lilies in the dark abyss—the kindness of nurses, the generosity of strangers, and the comfort of God.

One day Leah received a call from one of her daughters. "Emily!" Leah squealed with joy. Emily, adopted as a young child, had just received Leah's contact information from the adoption agency. Their restored relationship became another lily in our valley.

And then, the most important lily pushed its way through grief. Leah repented.

Members of the local United Pentecostal Church had spent hours at Leah's side, sharing a Bible study with her. The pastor came to her facility to baptize her in the name of Jesus. In August, she attended church in her wheelchair and received the Holy Spirit. Her personality changed. She recalled Bible stories she had learned as a child.

On a sunny September day, we drove to Yosemite National Park, where Leah stood beside the Merced River, "the River of Mercy," for a picture.

In October, Leah gathered her friends around her bed to pray. "Come on, let's go home," she said.

Before she left us on October 16, 2003, at the age of forty-five, I massaged between the rose tattoo and the unicorn tattoo on her shoulders and whispered, "God delights in mercy. You are a picture of His amazing grace. I will love you forever."

God did not heal Leah's body, but He saved her soul. That is the greatest miracle of all.

"Who *is* a God like unto thee, that pardoneth iniquity, and passeth by the transgression of the remnant of his heritage? he retaineth not his anger for ever, because he delighteth *in* mercy" (Micah 7:18).

Note: The doctors' names in this true story have been changed.

Run, James, Run

As told by James Fowler

I felt like nothing—a big fat zero. Well, maybe not even that. More like **0**. ^{Little, insignificant. Out of synch.} Insecurity, rejection, drugs, homelessness, jail—life had ripped everything of value away from me.

When I was a preteen, my family attended a United Pentecostal Church for about two years. I was baptized in the name of Jesus and received the Holy Ghost.

Then everything blew up . . . again. We stopped going to church. My parents divorced for the second time. My dad's national guard division was activated. The uncertainty of military life overwhelmed me. My mother's issues added to the instability of our home. She, my two younger brothers, and I moved from house to house, city to city. I don't remember how many schools I attended.

When I was fifteen, my dad was deployed to Iraq. I was devastated. Life with Mom deteriorated. Chaos. Fights. Heartache.

Run, James, run!

I went to live with my dad's sister. She tried to help me, but I was out of control—smoking, drinking, carousing. I was still enrolled in school, but I skipped more than I went.

When Dad came home from Iraq, I went to live with him. He bought me a car, and I relished the freedom.

One evening I drove up in front of Dad's house and fell asleep before I put the car in park. My relaxed foot hit the accelerator. One, two, three, four, five, six, seven cars ping ponged across the street as my car batted them.

The day I turned eighteen, I moved out of Dad's house and in with a roommate. The downward spiral continued down, down,

down into the dungeon of drugs. I was seeking escape, but I found bondage. Marijuana turned into cocaine, then pills, and eventually heroin. I was in and out of jail. Homeless. Begging for money to buy drugs.

About the time I turned twenty-three, I was arrested for possession of fourteen pills. In Alabama each pill is a felony, a daunting charge. My prospects were bleak.

So goes the life of a young man with nothing to lose. I wanted to show the world how much nothing I was. "Much nothing?" An oxymoron. That's what my life was: an oxymoron. It made as much sense as a "living death." In fact, it was a living death. More friends than I wanted to count died of overdoses.

Run, James, run.

I moved from Birmingham to Mobile and got a good job at Ruth Chris, an up-scale restaurant. I took a shower, got a haircut, and put on a sharp uniform. Drugs? I dropped everything but marijuana . . . at least from all appearances. In the background, it was a different story. Eventually, I could hide my addiction no longer.

One day when I was twenty-four, a buddy called. "James, you oughta come to Colorado. I'm raising weed . . . legally. Well, mostly legally. Smokin' all I want. You can get a job out here and live the high life."

Run, James, run.

What have I got to lose? More than I realized. Again, I ran; rather I rode a bus to Pueblo, Colorado.

My run to Colorado was not quite as fast as previous runs. I was dragging a lot of baggage: addiction, felony charges, hopelessness.

My buddy and I started watching weird videos on You Tube about the end of the world. Paranoia from the drugs and conviction from God unsettled me. *What if the world is about to end? What if my life is about to end?* I could not stop thinking about my dead buddies. Memories of what I had learned and experienced at church those two preteen years flooded my mind.

The Spirit of God wooed me. "Run, James, run. Run to Me."

One evening I stepped out onto the porch of a neighbor's house. I lifted my hands and my soul up to God. His Spirit washed away the fear, the guilt, the hopelessness, as I spoke once again in that heavenly language. He lifted me out of the pit of drugs and despair.

After that soul cleansing, I went back into the house where my buddy and I lived. I picked up my battered Bible, which I had ignored for years. It fell open to Acts 2:17: "And it shall come to pass in the last days, saith God, I will pour out of *my* Spirit upon all flesh."

I called my dad. He said, "Call the church."

I called Christian Growth Center and asked if someone could pick me up for church. They did. At this writing four years later, my record has been expunged in Alabama and in Heaven. I am married to a beautiful, godly young lady, have a steady job, and am picking up others to bring them to church. I know now that I was never "nothing." I am and always have been something—a child of God.

"He brought me up also out of an horrible pit, out of the miry clay, and set my feet upon a rock, *and* established my goings" (Psalm 40:2).

The Prayer Cloud

As told by Fabian Gray

Fabian has been shot! Call 911! He's been shot in the head!" Bullets blasted the house as a car roared by. The party came to a chilling halt.

Fabian sat on the couch hearing the screams but feeling neither panic nor pain. He just sat there.

How does a twenty-nine-year-old who was born again at fourteen and totally sold out to God throughout high school end up at a drug party with a bullet through the top of his head? Little by little—making a wrong friend, moving from the center of the church to the peripheral, then to the clubs. Wrong attitude. Wrong friends. Wrong environment. Wrong thinking. "I messed up, so I might as well give up." He traded his church family for the cocaine circle.

But this night on the couch in his friend's house, Fabian was not reviewing his life. His brain was traumatized. His mind was blank. He simply sat there as the partiers frantically scurried between the bathroom destroying evidence and the window watching. *Who will come first, the police or the ambulance?* They needed help. They feared interrogation. Fabian just sat there.

The next thing he remembers is the paramedics shining a light in his eyes before he passed out. The doctors at Parkview Hospital in Pueblo, Colorado, gave him a 30-percent chance of surviving the life flight to Swedish Hospital in Denver. He survived.

The prayer grapevine buzzed around the world. Prayers ascended to the throne.

The doctors told his parents, "If he lives, he will be a vegetable. There is too much brain damage for him to recover." Fabian lived.

In the ICU cubicle Tim and Lora Gray gasped when they saw the unrecognizable form on the hospital bed. Their son's head was swathed in bandages. He was shackled to the bed by tubes hooked to beeping machines. Thus began their vigil at his bedside.

The doctors revised their prognosis. "Fabian is going to be totally paralyzed on his left side."

The fourth day when the Grays walked into ICU, Lora saw a cloud filling Fabian's cubicle. Tiny beams of light shot from the cloud over his bed, hitting him from his head to his feet.

She pointed up. "Babe! Look! Look up!"

Fabian's dad looked up and shrugged. "What? What are you talking about?"

"Don't you see it?" she asked. "It is a cloud of prayers. The prayers being prayed for Fabian are filling this room." Lora watched as the light outlined the sliding doors and radiated out into the ICU unit.

From that time Fabian slowly progressed. His eyes straightened. His arms moved.

Two doors down a lady lay dying. Her family had given up hope. Two days after Lora saw the prayer cloud, this lady's son stood outside her cubicle with a suitcase. Before Lora could voice her sympathy, the son turned to her. "You won't believe this! My mother is going home. It's a miracle!"

Lora rejoiced. The light from the prayers of Fabian's friends and family had spread. God's power had not been confined to one cubicle.

Meanwhile, Fabian heard everything that was said, even though he could not respond. Before he could communicate with anyone else, he talked to God—a broken prodigal on his way home. With each feeble step he took, Heaven rejoiced.

The journey was long. After three months in the hospital and rehab, Fabian was released to go home as an outpatient. His parents dropped everything and dedicated themselves to their son's care. While Fabian was still in a wheelchair, they took him to church.

At this writing Fabian Gray is married, self-employed doing construction work, and a faithful member of Christian Growth Center. Every step, every word, every day, he is a living miracle. His advice to young people: If you mess up, don't give up. Someone is praying for you.

"Then hear thou in heaven their prayer and their supplication, and maintain their cause" (I Kings 8:45).

To Hell and Back

Submitted by Sherii Parrett

Valentine Day 1981 started like any other day. I woke up. Got dressed. Went to school. That evening with my friends, I attended a rock concert by April Wine and Lover Boy. There, everything normal evaporated. I overdosed and went to hell!

Acid was our favorite concert drug. It is a hallucinogenic drug that causes every ray or sparkle of light to intensify until it feels the user is riding it. Sounds at a concert become part of the otherworld. When the effects peak, the trip revolves around whatever one sees or hears. Walking on a purple beam of light is just as real as walking on a gravel road.

My friend and I decided to split one hit of LSD 25. However, when her boyfriend heard about our plans, he got mad. So, being the good friend that she was, my friend gave me her half. I was 5' 2" and weighed 98 pounds. A quarter of a hit was excessive for my weight and frame.

By the time Lover Boy's "Teenage Overdose" played, I was tripping.

Everyone with me took on a demonic form. Some took on several. Each sin manifested itself as a different demon. The demons haunted me. "We have been sent to destroy you. It's too late for you! You're going to die. You're going to hell!" I believed every word. It seemed like this went on for hours.

I cried out the names of the individuals the demons were speaking through. I screamed at my brother, "Billy! Billy!" hoping I could see the real Billy, not the grotesque demon. When Billy spoke, I saw him, but when he stopped speaking, his demons cried out again. I kept trying to get those with me to talk so the demons could not speak through them.

Then there was a shift. No longer were the demons tormenting me. They were being tormented with me. We were all dead.

We walked down ramps toward a pit of flames and noise, squeezed in and shoved by the teeming multitude going down, down, down. Screams. Shouts. Shrieking. Panic-stricken, I looked for a way out but couldn't turn around. No way out.

Suddenly, I was in an abyss. Cut off. Darkness. Flames. Smells. No escape. Memories of my sister Tracy telling me about Heaven stabbed me. Regrets tormented me. Hopelessness smothered me. The darkness consumed me. No escape.

In the real world, I had lost consciousness. My friend Frank carried me out of the concert.

"What are we going to do with Sherii?" My friends, who were high themselves, were afraid to take me to the hospital because they could have been arrested.

Frank decided, "We'll take her home. Tracy will know what to do. She talks to God all the time. God will listen to her."

As soon as Tracy realized what had happened, she laid her hands on me and commanded, "Wake up! In Jesus name!"

Immediately, I was out of hell. At that second, I was completely sober.

The effects of LSD 25 do not go away in a moment. Often, it takes a day or two for an amount less than what I took to leave the body's system. While it is in the system, the hallucinations remain. But, when my sister prayed, I was immediately 100-percent sober.

"Take me to the church," I begged. I poured out my experience to those around me. I described their spirits which I had seen. I urged them to repent, be baptized in Jesus' name, and receive the Holy Ghost. "Hell is real! You don't want to go there!"

The next day my mother, my brothers, my aunt, my sister, her boyfriend, her best friend, my friend and her boyfriend, and several other friends went to church with me. We were all baptized in Jesus name, February 15, 1981. Today I am a licensed UPCI minister, a pastor's wife, and a conference speaker, ministering to prisoners and involved in numerous other ministries. From the age of eight, I have been an addict— first addicted to alcohol, then drugs. I am still an addict, but now I am addicted to the ministry of the saints.

What if my sister had not had a prayer life? What if she had not witnessed to me and my friends? This story could have been so different. I could have stayed in hell.

"And others save with fear, pulling *them* out of the fire" (Jude 1:23).

MIRACLES OF HEALING

A Double Miracle

Submitted by John Chance

It was revival time at Calvary United Pentecostal Church of Jonesboro, Arkansas, Sunday morning 2009. A guest, Evelyn Weatherford, stood next to her mother-in-law as the altar call was made. Background music played. Conviction lingered. Whispered prayers of intercession wrapped around the sanctuary.

Evangelist Robert Tisdale asked, "Does anyone need God to touch you? Does anyone need the Holy Ghost?"

Evelyn joined others on the life-changing walk from pew to altar. Saints gathered around. Cries of repentance and worship ascended to the throne room.

As Pastor John Chance started across the sanctuary to pray with someone, the evangelist instructed the seekers, "As a show of faith of what God is about to do for you, raise your hands toward Heaven and begin to pray."

With eyes closed and tears flowing, Evelyn quickly raised her left arm. Her right arm lingered crookedly about shoulder height. For the first time Pastor Chance noticed Evelyn's withered right arm and hand. He wondered, *Has she had a stroke?* As he walked by Evelyn, her crooked arm straightened and shot straight up. Immediately, she started speaking in a heavenly language as she received the Holy Ghost.

After the service, the pastor and evangelist were amazed to learn that, some time before, Evelyn had been in a car accident. Her neck had been broken and her right side partially paralyzed. But that Sunday, when Evelyn raised her right hand as far as she could as a show of faith, God did what He does best. He performed a miracle. In fact, He performed a double miracle. He straightened her arm and saved her soul.

"Stretch forth thy hand. And [s]he did so: and [her] hand was restored whole as the other" (Luke 6:10).

A Healing Bolt

Submitted by Neva Limones

E cuador. Circa 1973. "Vilma Limones has had a stroke. The doctors have sent her home to die. She is totally bed-ridden." The shocking message spread through the headquarters church.

Vilma was a much loved, godly saint, a pastor's wife, and mother of seven children. The dedication of the Limones family was well known throughout Ecuador. Before moving to the city, they had faithfully walked miles to church through pouring rain or blistering heat, inky darkness or dawning light.

Word came to Missionaries Daniel and Joretta Scott. "Sister Vilma has asked for the elders of the church to come and pray for her." The missionaries asked Evangelist Scotty Teats, who had a unique faith ministry, to accompany them.

This godly trio climbed the stairs to the apartment over the headquarters church where the Limones family lived. As they gathered around the stricken saint, Samuel, one of the Limones's sons, sat at the foot of the bed holding his mother's foot.

Vilma's vocal cords were so damaged she could only articulate garbled sounds. But using her good hand and her awkward voice, she communicated to the missionary wife that she wanted her limp arm raised as she lifted her other arm to praise God. Joretta Scott held up her friend's flaccid arm, as Vilma raised the other. The believers bombarded Heaven. Their prayers saturated the atmosphere and ascended to the throne room. Suddenly, a bolt of power surged through the crippled body on the bed. The bolt hurled Samuel to the floor. The power of God energized the withered body. She jumped to her feet, praising God with a strong vibrant voice, waving both arms. No help needed. Thank You, Jesus!

She immediately returned to her daily duties caring for her family. A few years later the missionaries' daughter Neva married the Limones's son, Elias. At this writing, Vilma Limones is eighty-six years old, still on fire for God and electrifying the church with her testimony of the bolt from Heaven.

"Thus will I bless thee while I live: I will lift up my hands in thy name" (Psalm 63:4).

A Midnight Call

Submitted by Neva Limones

The ringing phone awakened Pastor Limones. He groaned and squinted. It was the middle of the night.

He picked up the handset. "Limones here."

"Chaplain Limones, there has been a tragic motorcycle-train accident." The half-awake man fumbled for his trousers as the voice on the other end of the line continued, "You are needed at the hospital STAT!"

As he sped toward the hospital, the pastor-chaplain recounted some of the many miracles he had witnessed while serving as a chaplain. It sounded like he needed another one. He prayed for divine intervention.

At the hospital, the distraught mother grabbed his arm. "They say there is no hope. My son is gone! But you must pray for him." She dragged him to the room where her son's battered and broken lifeless body lay.

Chaplain Limones's heart sank. It was evident the young man whose motorcycle had tangled with a train had lost the battle.

The mother yanked on the chaplain's sleeve. "Pray! You must pray!"

He assumed that she was Catholic and wanted him to pray for her son's soul. He turned to the mother, who was sobbing and wringing her hands, and said gently, "I will pray that God will strengthen and comfort you."

"No! No!" she protested. "You must pray for my son. He must not die! He must not!"

"But your son is . . ." He gulped and tried again. "His soul is gone—" Her harsh cries interrupted his soft words.

She shook her head wildly. "No! No! You must pray. You must pray!"

Taking a deep breath, Chaplain Limones laid his hands on the young man's head. He rebuked death in Jesus' name and commanded life to return to the broken body. They watched in amazement as the crushed chest slowly rose and fell again and again as breath entered his lungs.

Later as the weary chaplain drove toward home, he filled the car with praise. One more time God had miraculously intervened.

A few days later in the course of his duties, Chaplain Limones decided to check on the young man. When he inquired for the room number, he was told, "Oh, he's been released to rehab."

Chaplain Josias Limones was not the only one who answered that midnight call.

"For I will restore health unto thee, and I will heal thee of thy wounds, saith the LORD" (Jeremiah 30:17).

A Miracle in the Nursery

Submitted by Denzil Holman

On November 17, 1964, my wife was admitted to the Methodist Hospital for what we assumed would be a normal birth. When our oldest son Randy was born, for a few minutes everything seemed normal. Then in a few short breaths, disaster disrupted our serene world. Our newborn was gasping for every breath. His color was an ashen grey.

The doctors diagnosed him with Hyaline Membrane, the same disease that took the life of the son of President John F. Kennedy.

I was a young man with the call of God to the ministry, trying to find the will of God for our lives. We were living in Louisville, Kentucky, where we had recently moved. We had no relatives in Kentucky and were alone in our crisis, except for the pastor and friends from the United Pentecostal Church we attended.

After the birth, Doctor Churney told us, "Your son will not live more than seventy-two hours. One of his lungs is filled with the membrane, and the other lung is 75-percent filled." We were stunned speechless. He continued, "I don't think you understood what I said. Your son is going to die."

When I looked through the nursery window at our little boy in an incubator, his tiny chest was heaving nearly to his backbone. He gasped for every tortured breath.

People in our home church in Phoenix prayed. People in Louisville prayed. Several days passed. My wife was released and went home. Our baby boy did not. But he was still breathing.

One day after work, I stopped by the hospital and walked to the nursery window. What had happened? Our baby's breathing was normal. His color was a healthy pink. There had been an enormous change. God had healed him.

After Randy was released, we took him to Doctor Churney several times for checkups. Each time we heard the nurses telling each other, "That miracle baby is here."

At this writing Randy is fifty-four years old, married, and a grandpa. He has never had any more health issues from Hyaline Membrane.

"The Spirit of God hath made me, and the breath of the Almighty hath given me life" (Job 33:4).

A Prayer Meeting in the Front Lawn

By Barbara Westberg

It was 1946 in Tiawah, Oklahoma, a minute dot on the map. Our family of four lived in a cracker-box house across the gravel road from First Apostolic Church, the white country church we attended.

As a 7-year-old girl, I was not aware of the tension and fear radiating in our home. My younger sister was even less cognizant of the situation. I did know that my mother had been going to the doctor a lot, and she had not been going to church. Both were unusual.

One Sunday after morning worship, the entire congregation from our church walked across the gravel road to our house. Our pastor, C. A. Nelson, my dad, and perhaps a couple of other elders went inside. Everyone else stayed in the front yard and prayed.

A few days later my mother returned to the doctor. She came home rejoicing. "The test was negative," she told my dad and everyone who would listen.

Much later I learned that my mother had been diagnosed with tuberculosis. In those days people with TB were confined (sentenced? ordered?) to a sanitarium, where they got lots of sunshine, rest, and a healthy diet. Some patients stayed for months, even years. It was the only known treatment. Before the church prayed that Sunday, the doctor had told my mother, "Marcella, if this next test is positive, you have no choice. You must go to a sanitarium for treatment. You are contagious."

Of course, my parents were devastated. How could my dad, who worked forty-eight hours a week for our family to survive, take care of two little girls? What would happen to us? To their marriage? To their walk with God? But all that uncertainty and fear was swept away that Sunday by a front yard prayer meeting.

Almost forty years later, my mother applied for a job at a school cafeteria. She was given a physical, including a chest X-ray. The technician told her, "Mrs. Hoselton, you have had TB. Your lungs are scarred." That was not news to her, but it was a reminder of the Sunday when the saints gathered for a prayer meeting on the front lawn.

"Prayer was made without ceasing of the church unto God for [her]" (Acts 12:5).

A Real-Life Illustration

As told by Sandra Elder

My husband came out of the bathroom squinting. "Sandra, something is wrong with my right eye. I can't see out of it."

I took a deep breath. "Carl, are you sure? Surely not. Check again."

He was sure. He had no vision in his right eye.

As we did about everything, we prayed. My pastor-husband went about his daily activities, worked, preached, and prayed. I cared for our home and the saints and prayed. Together we prayed. Separately we prayed.

A few days later, Carl made an appointment with an ophthalmologist that we had consulted in the past. When Carl was called back to see the doctor, I waited. When he returned, I knew by the look on his face that the news was not good.

On the way home he told me, "The doctor said a blood vessel has ruptured in that eye. The damage is extensive. It cannot be repaired. I will be blind in that eye for the rest of my life."

Carl was not surprised, but he had hoped for a better prognosis—corrective glasses or surgery or something. The doctor's words wiped out all hope of medical technology helping him. He did not whine or complain, but often I saw him covering his left eye to check the right one. No change. No vision. We continued to pray "not my will, but Thine be done," as we praised God for Carl's remaining vision.

Not long after the doctor's visit, we traveled to California to the No Limits conference. The first evening of the conference, I sat by my husband on the end of the second row by the aisle, Several members of our family sat with us.

The evening speaker, Randy Keys, preached an anointed message on God's healing power. He related the account of a minister in a foreign country praying for a blind man. The presence of the Lord saturated the congregation. Shaking under the anointing of the Holy Ghost, Brother Keys stepped off the platform and started down the aisle, preaching as he walked. He stopped by us. With no awareness of the doctor's findings, Brother Keys laid his hand on my husband's chest illustrating the miracle in a faraway land. With anointing and authority, he spoke healing over Carl.

An electrical current shot down the pew. Carl rolled his head back and forth. He blinked. He blinked again. He covered his good eye and read the words on the screen with his "blind" eye. He leaned over to me, "Sandra, God just healed me!"

During the altar service, Carl shared what had happened with our son Paul. Word spread. Carl was asked to testify. He went to the pulpit and gave witness to the miraculous healing power of God. What a way to end a service! What a way to start a conference!

We returned home and made an appointment with the doctor to get documentation of our miracle. This time I went into the consultation room with my husband. First, the nurse examined Carl's vision. When he witnessed to her about his healing, she rejoiced.

When the doctor came in, Carl told him, "My vision is clear. God has healed my eye." As he testified about the miraculous power of God, the doctor's face tightened and darkened. His whole demeanor shouted unbelief. Through tight lips, he ordered tests. Every test proved the vision in Carl's right eye was 20/20. Sad to say, that doctor never acknowledged that a miracle had happened. He marked Carl off his patients' list and refused to see him again.

Carl had clear vision in that eye until the day he died.

"The power of the Lord was *present* to heal [him]" (Luke 5:17).

A Sacrifice of Praise

By Shannon McCoy

May 2, 2001. I was forty-one weeks pregnant and scheduled for a routine induction as my little girl, Rebekah, was not making any effort to come on her own. It had been a normal pregnancy—nothing alarming.

When the hospital had a bed for me, they called and suggested that we go to dinner before checking in since I would be in labor several hours. But my husband, Chris, was anxious. "Let's skip dinner and go straight to the hospital before an emergency takes our bed." Little did we know that we would be the emergency.

The nurses hooked me up to the necessary monitors. Nurse Sharon frowned. They could not find the baby's heartbeat. "Turn over, Shannon," she ordered gently.

I turned. She worried her lips. She moved the monitor. A few heartbeats, then silence.

One of the nurses alerted the nurses' station. Another nurse walked in. They talked in nurse-code. They thought the cord had wrapped about the baby's neck. They did an exam. Normal.

Intensity increased.

They slapped an oxygen mask on my face. "Relax, Shannon. Breathe so the baby can get oxygen." I was terrified. Breathing calmly was a struggle.

"Page her O.B. doctors," Sharon ordered.

My doctors were walking to their cars when their pagers sounded. They ran back into the hospital and were directed to my room. The nurses were desperately trying to find a heartbeat on the monitor.

Doctor Shakespeare instructed, "We need to do a blood gas check on the baby. We have to know if she is getting any oxygen."

The test came back normal.

Pandemonium set in. The nurses were barking orders to the operating room. My family was in and out my room. My sister, Kimmie, called a lady in our church. "Something's wrong with the baby. Please, start a prayer chain now."

Phones rang. Saints dropped to their knees. Others rushed to the hospital.

Dr. Shakespeare told Chris, "We have to take the baby by emergency C-section, or she won't make it. We don't know what's wrong, but she's dying!"

Chris was still signing the consent form as my bed was wheeled toward surgery. I grabbed his hand and begged. "Please don't leave me!"

A nurse ripped our hands apart, shouting, "We don't have time for this!"

As they hooked me up to IVs, someone declared, "There is no heartbeat."

In two minutes, they prepped me for surgery, put me under a general anesthesia, cut me open, and pulled Rebekah out. All in 120 seconds! My baby was pale, floppy, and did not have a pulse. The surgeon was ready to pronounce her dead.

"Let me try!" A nurse grabbed the baby and found a tiny pulse. They rushed her across the hall to NICU. They ran a tube down her throat and in her navel, inserted IVs, put a pulse sock and leads on her, and added a urine bag. My baby started fighting. She pulled out the tube. They restrained her tiny hand and reinserted the tube.

The fight for life was on. For seven days she teetered between life and death. They ran every test imaginable on her, me, and the placenta, trying to find out what had happened. Every test came back normal or negative. No answers.

I was exhausted.

Our church was in revival. I battled between going to church for strength or to the hospital to sit with our baby.

Chris made the decision for me. "Let's go to church, then we can spend the rest of the night at the hospital if you want."

At church the evangelist sang and sang and sang. And sang some more. I was frustrated and worried and tired. I was present physically, but not mentally. Since the singing went on and on, I decided I might as well get on board with the worship. A spirit of intercession came over the congregation. We wept and prayed.

Suddenly a holy hush silenced everyone. A message in tongues came forth. I will never forget the interpretation. "Fear not! This night I will raise up your child. Your child is in My hands. Because of your faithfulness to Me, I will show my love to you and heal her."

I cannot express my feelings. Even now eighteen years later, I weep as I write. We were given an anointed prayer cloth and instructed to wipe it one time across her forehead.

When we entered NICU, our little miracle was sound asleep and smiling. My husband wiped the prayer cloth across Rebekah's forehead.

The IV was missing from her left hand. The nurse explained, "The site closed. She doesn't need the IV anymore."

"What time did this happened?" I asked.

"About 6:30 this evening." That was the exact moment we decided to go to church. Even when I did not know it, God was working.

As the respiratory therapist walked by, Chris asked, "Our baby's monitor looks funny. What does that mean?"

The RT looked puzzled. "That's normal. That's how it is supposed to look."

Three days later the hospital staff waved good-bye to our baby as she was released. Over and over they marveled, "We don't know what happened! She is completely changed."

We smiled into the pink face of our baby daughter as her chest rose and fell in a natural rhythm. "We know exactly what happened," we assured them. But God. . . .

What was the song Evangelist Tony Peterson was singing? "I exalt Thee, O Lord." That night I learned what it means to offer a sacrifice of praise.

"By him therefore let us offer the sacrifice of praise to God continually, that is, the fruit of our lips giving thanks to his name" (Hebrews 13:15).

A Sinner's Cry

Submitted by Karen Brown

The summer of 1977 was stressful for our family. My mother-in-law, Inez, had stage 4 colon cancer. We were her primary caregivers. When her condition worsened, she was admitted to the hospital in Stillwater, Oklahoma.

During this time my 6-month-old daughter, Hannah, broke out in a rash. I took her to the health department, suspecting that it was chicken pox or a childhood disease.

The nurse looked at the rash and did a cursory exam. "You need to see your pediatrician. Give me his name. I will call and get you in as soon as possible."

The doctor's staff worked us in immediately. He frowned as he examined Hannah. "This looks like Rocky Mountain Spotted Fever. Has she been bitten by a tick?"

My heart sank. "Yes. A few days ago."

"Take her to the hospital now for more tests. Several people have died from Rocky Mountain Fever this summer. Just a week ago a baby died."

Was he saying that my baby had only a week to live? I panicked. My mother-in-law was in the hospital dying, and now my baby was dying! My husband was out of town, and it would take time to contact him.

After the tests at the hospital were completed, the intern instructed, "Take your baby home. The doctor will call you when we get the results."

As I drove toward my mother-in-law's house, tears streamed down my face. The road was a gray blur. The drive seemed endless, although it was only a couple of miles. I sobbed and prayed to the God I only knew peripherally through my in-laws' relationship with Him. I did not have their faith. *How could I*

muster up enough faith when I was not living for God? People
with that kind of faith got it from years of walking with God.
Would God even listen to a sinner like me?

At home, the wait started. Waiting for the call. Waiting for
my husband to get home. Waiting and praying to the best of my
ability.

Finally, the phone rang. Hannah did not have Rocky
Mountain Spotted Fever, but she did have an extremely low
blood platelet count. "Do not let her bump herself, as bleeding
can be a problem."

Tears of relief and anxiety mixed. I admitted, "She just
bumped her head on the coffee table."

"Bring her back to the clinic now," the doctor ordered.

For months we kept a close watch on Hannah, returning to
the hospital for frequent blood tests. Every time her blood count
dropped, she broke out, but her symptoms had nothing to do
with Rocky Mountain Spotted Fever. She eventually grew out
of it.

The doctors were puzzled. The rash had looked exactly like
RMSF. The grandson of a friend recently contacted this dreaded
fever. His rash looked exactly like Hannah's.

Did Hannah have RMSF? I do not know. I do know that God
heard this desperate sinner's cry and turned this mother's heart
to Him. Isn't that the greatest miracle of all?

"So that they cause the cry of the poor to come unto him, and
he heareth the cry of the afflicted" (Job 34:28).

A Strange Pocket

Submitted by Tashia Smith

Giggles. Shouts. Songs. The campground was filled with happy sounds. I enjoyed every minute of our annual children's summer camp—fixing fancy Pentecostal hairdos, finding lost shoes, and hugging little homesick girls.

At camp 2015, my daughter four-year-old Gabriella was quieter than normal and a bit clingy, but I figured it was because of the boisterous atmosphere. She was not eating much, but I assumed that was because camp food is never quite as good as Mom's. She was tired and draggy, but I reasoned that was because of the late nights. This went on for four days until time to go home.

The last morning at breakfast, she refused to eat a bite. I wrapped my arm around her and patted her side.

She screamed in agony.

I froze. Then I gently picked her up and rushed her to the camp EMT and nurse.

A few minutes later they agreed, "We are 99-percent sure it is her appendix. You need to get her to the doctor immediately."

My husband and I had brought the musical instruments and sound system from our church in Hutchinson, Kansas, to the campground. It was time to close the camp and return the equipment to church for service the next day. When it was evident that we had an emergency on our hands, our friends pitched in to load the equipment and our luggage. In fifteen minutes, everything was in the van. That in itself was a miracle.

Before we pulled out the campground, our pastor, Nathan Karriker, prayed with us. As we raced for the urgent care in Hutchinson, phones around the country rang. The message went out, "Pray for Gabriella." Prayers ascended focused the throne.

At 11:00 my husband dropped Gabriella and I off at urgent care and went to the church to unload. "I'll be back as soon as possible," he promised.

The staff at the clinic asked a few questions, then decided, "We can't take care of her here. Take her across the street to the hospital." So, I carried her in my arms across the street, all the while praying for God to intervene.

It had been two and one-half hours since I had patted Gabriella's side.

While the emergency room doctor examined her, the nurses hooked up an IV. Following the doctor's orders, they gave her a dose of morphine. The doctor told us, "We have called for medical transport to take your daughter to the hospital in Wichita."

For two hours we sat beside our pale, comatose little girl in a sterile ER cubicle and prayed. Agonizing every minute.

Finally, the medical transport arrived. At 1:30 I climbed into the ambulance with Gabriella and an EMT. My husband followed in our car. Every few miles, I gritted my teeth to keep from screaming, "Are we there yet? Can't you go any faster?"

At the Wichita hospital they took a sonagram. The results came back . . . inconclusive. Her appendix may have already ruptured; it may be seeping, or there might be nothing wrong.

The doctor came in. She told us, "We have to do surgery. Every minute counts. We can't take a chance that the appendix will rupture."

Little did anyone know, but Gabriella's appendix had ruptured.

Surgery was scheduled for 6:30 that evening, but one emergency after another (greater than ours?) pushed ahead of us.

Finally, at 11:30 our baby was rolled into the operating room. A long, agonizing hour later, the surgeon stepped into the waiting room. "You should be planning a funeral," he said. What a way to start a conversation with frightened parents! He continued, "Your daughter should be septic, but she is not. Her appendix has ruptured. But somehow, I don't understand how, her body created a hard pocket that contained the infection. When she was born, her appendix grew backward and tucked up instead of hanging down. Her large intestine, ovary, and abdominal wall glued together and created a pocket that sealed the infection off from the rest of her body."

He knocked the wall to illustrate what they had found in our baby's body. "The pocket is so hard that we had to drill into it to insert a tube to drain the infection. I don't understand how this could happen. In situations like this there is only a 1- to 3-percent chance the patient will survive."

I said, "We understand, doctor. God did it!" We took deep breaths and wiped our tears.

The doctor did not disagree. "She will probably be in the hospital a week. We are putting in a pic-line that she will need for two weeks. After that we will do surgery again to remove the damaged appendix."

One week in the hospital was shortened to three days. She told the nurses over and over, "God did it. He healed me."

She continued antibiotics at home for two weeks through her pic-line by IV. Our little girl's color and sparkle returned.

Two weeks later Gabriella was again rolled into the operating room. The doctor came out smiling. "She'll be fine. All her organs had returned to their normal position. The infection is gone!"

Fast forward one year. Five-year-old Gabriella stood before her friends at children's camp and testified about her personal miracle of the strange pocket.

"And they were all amazed, and they glorified God, and were filled with fear, saying, We have seen strange things to day" (Luke 5:26).

Added Years

Submitted by Denzil Holman

It was September 1957. I was sixteen years old and a senior in high school. My dad was bi-vocational, pastoring a church in Canton, Ohio, and working the midnight shift as a welder for E. W. Bliss Company. We were constructing the first phase of a new church building, a 36' x 68' basement built of concrete blocks. It was back-breaking, sweat-producing work.

One Saturday morning Dad came in from work and woke me up. "We only have six rows left to complete the north wall. Let's get it done today."

Wayne Jackson joined our meager work crew. As the last block was cemented into place, my forty-year-old dad collapsed. A heart attack.

He survived that one, but soon was back in the hospital. Saturday morning the phone rang. I answered. "Son, I am coming home by ambulance. The hospital does not want to release me, but I am coming anyway. I have some final instructions for my family and the church."

At home we gathered around our dying dad's bed. I assumed that, as the oldest of four children, I would have to quit school to support my family.

After Dad gave us his instruction, he told my mother, "Call the saints. I have a few admonishments to leave with them. I would like for us to take communion."

When we left the room, Dad turned his face to the wall and prayed. "God, please spare me to raise my children."

That evening the church gathered. Dad, dressed in pajamas and a robe, walked the few feet from our home to the church. He stood behind the pulpit for what he felt was his last time. His countenance was pasty white. He gasped for breath as he spoke a few words of pastoral exhortation.

During the service, two minister friends arrived. As they prayed for my dad, shock waves of God's Spirit went through the building. Dad's countenance changed to a rosy pink. He was instantly healed.

A couple of years later, my baby sister was born. Dad and Mom raised my siblings. The church building was finished, and the congregation grew. I entered the ministry, and Dad preached in the church I pastored in Norfolk, Virginia. Dad lived to see his heart's desires. Just like Hezekiah, God added another fifteen years to Dad's life.

"He asked life of thee, *and* thou gavest *it* him, *even* length of days . . . (Psalm 21:4).

All Things Well

By Teresa Bohannon

I want to testify!

Our grandson, Lincoln Jude Bohannon, was born September 11, 2019. Three months later he was diagnosed with a form of hydrocephalus—fluid buildup on the brain causing his head to swell. This was not what we wanted to hear. We started ringing family and friends' phones and the prayer bells of Heaven.

In February he had brain surgery. The neurosurgeon, supported by much prayer, performed an Endoscopic Third Ventriculostomy—a hole created through a ventricle to allow the fluid to drain. Just the thought of the procedure struck pain to our hearts, but we grasped God's hand and bent His ear. The operation went smoothly, we thought.

But a week later Lincoln was back in the hospital with pneumonia and several viruses. It was touch and go. We almost lost our baby. For a week we rode an emotional roller-coaster. Our intercession turned to praise when Jesus touched our baby, and Lincoln was released from the hospital.

I had gone with Jason and Jenn (Lincoln's parents) to Linc's first visit with the neuro ophthalmologist, the only doctor of this type south of Los Angeles and west of Phoenix. At that time, he had said that our baby was likely facing eye surgery and would need corrective glasses. He recommended putting a patch over one of Lincoln's eyes and rotating it each day until his next visit.

In September, Lincoln went for a one-year physical with his pediatrician and a six-month follow-up with his neurosurgeon. Each doctor was totally amazed at his progress. The follow-up MRI on his head showed no problems. Since then he has had no seizures, nothing that usually accompanies this problem. The neurosurgeon said he rarely sees a perfect case, but this is one! The pediatrician said she was blown away. Every concern she had was gone.

At the six-month follow-up with the neuro ophthalmologist, he asked Lincoln's parents, "Have you been patching his eye?"

Lincoln's mother replied, "Yes."

The doctor smiled. "I am amazed. His right eye is fine. The left one, which I was most concerned about, is much stronger. Your baby does not need surgery or corrective glasses. I would like to see him in six months to re-evaluate."

All doctors concurred our grandson was meeting and exceeding every milestone for his age, way beyond anything they expected. At this writing, he is starting to talk, pulls up, and takes a few steps. Soon he will be walking. His head is slightly enlarged, but not like they expected it to be. They believe he will "grow into his head," meaning his body will catch up with his head. He is the happiest little guy, always smiling.

God does all things well.

"And [they] were beyond measure astonished, saying, He hath done all things well" (Mark 7:37).

An Eyewitness Account

By Richard M. Davis

I cannot recall the exact year, but it must have been about 1977. It was Saturday and the day before Easter.

My wife and I had gone to visit her parents who were pastoring in Gadsden, Alabama. On that Saturday, a family from the church stopped by my in-laws' home. As they were getting ready to leave, six-year-old Shanna decided to get into the car while everyone else was gathered on the front porch.

Suddenly, Shanna knocked the car gearshift into neutral, and the car rolled backwards toward the street below. It all happened so quickly it was as if we were momentarily frozen in time. We saw what was happening but seemed unable to move—at least not quickly enough. As we ran toward the rolling car, the most dreadful thing happened: in fear, Shanna jumped out of the driver's open door.

Had Shanna completely cleared the car, it would have been a good thing, but, unfortunately, she did not clear the vehicle. The window crank handle caught her dress and dragged her alongside the rolling vehicle toward the street.

When the rear wheels of the car reached the street, the front wheels turned. A front tire rolled directly across the abdomen of little Shanna. We watched in horror as we sprinted toward her and the car, which had cleared her body.

Someone captured and commandeered the runaway vehicle while another scooped up the little limp body of Shanna. We breathed, screamed, and pled the name of Jesus Christ. Despite our prayers, a sick sense of helplessness swept over me. I knew what I had just witnessed. I envisioned the worst imaginable outcome.

What happened next was probably the least wise thing we did that day. Instead of calling for an ambulance, we gathered Shanna and several others into our car and sped toward the hospital, ten minutes away. Looking back, we know it would have been best to call for medical assistance, but, in our panicked state of mind, we wanted to get Shanna to the hospital as quickly as possible. We called on Jesus all the way!

At the emergency waiting room, a small crowd of somber, but prayerful believers gathered. For a couple of hours, we paced, prayed, and waited to hear news of Shanna's condition. To say I felt a sense of surging faith would be far less than honest. I knew what I had witnessed with my own eyes. The heavy front end of a sixties-model vehicle had rolled directly across that child's torso. I could only imagine the extent of the internal organ destruction she had suffered.

Finally, the attending physician came out into the waiting room. The news was shocking but thrilling. They were releasing Shanna. After a thorough examination, they had discovered no internal bleeding, no damage to the internal organs, no broken bones—she was fine and being discharged.

I watched with amazement the next morning as Shanna ran and played with the other children dressed in their beautiful Easter outfits. I knew without doubt we had received a miracle!

The skeptic who was not there will calculate all the possible reasons why more severe injuries were avoided. Perhaps her body fell into a slight depression in the driveway, allowing the extreme weight of the car to avoid direct contact. The skeptic will just assume there was a freakish or unusual circumstance that could explain her lack of injury. But I was there! I know what I saw. It was without question the most painful, horrible thing I have ever witnessed. I am no skeptic. I am a believer in the miraculous hand of the Almighty. I will always praise and worship my God for our Easter miracle.

"Verily, verily, I say unto thee, We speak that we do know, and testify that we have seen" (John 3:11).

An Unexpected Interruption

Submitted by Shelly O'Leary

Opening night 2017. Junior camp in Shawano, Wisconsin. *Hallelujahs* rocked the sanctuary as students and staff joined our praise team singing "Dancing Generation." I was excited to be on the staff, both as a member of the praise team and a teacher. I looked forward to meeting my students the next morning.

Then it happened . . . an unexpected interruption.

Suddenly, amid the ringing hallelujahs, I collapsed onto my back, hitting my head so hard it bounced on the wooden platform. My teeth sank through my lip, creating a bloody mess and a choking hazard. Some thought I was slain in the Spirit, but a nurse ran forward to check my pulse. I had none.

My heart had stopped.

The nurse yelled for help. Within seconds, nurses and EMTs from the congregation joined her. Someone called 911. The medical team took turns administering chest compressions non-stop. To prevent pandemonium, the worship leader led the rest of the praise team, students, and adults to another building. Everyone prayed. A spirit of intercession swept the campground. "Jesus! Jesus! Help us!" Children raised their hands toward the building where I lay unresponsive. No pulse. No breath. No life.

Word spread quickly. At my home church, the assistant pastor broke into the Monday night prayer meeting to announce that I needed urgent prayer. My pastor's wife called my husband, "Josh, Shelly collapsed. We have called for an ambulance." She wanted him to know the situation was urgent enough to make the 2-hour drive but did not want him to be so concerned he would not drive safely.

Minutes passed—five, six, eight, ten, twelve. Every minute the urgency increased. Prayers escalated.

The first responder to arrive on the scene lived only a mile from the campgrounds. He had a defibrillator with him, but lacked the other basic supplies needed. As he was not familiar with administering care in cardiac arrest situations, the nurses insisted on taking care of me. The first two shocks they administered did not revive me. To everyone's relief, the third one did. Prayers continued.

When the ambulance arrived, I had been without pulse and breath for fifteen minutes. I was loaded on a gurney, frantically attended to by a different team of professionals. As the nurses, my pastor, his wife, and other camp staffers watched the ambulance drive away, a new concern settled in. *What if their chest compressions had kept blood flowing to my heart only to leave me brain damaged?* Effectual fervent prayers bombarded God's throne.

At the local hospital it was clear that I needed more care than the small-town facility could offer. I was loaded into a helicopter, headed for a larger hospital with a skilled cardiology team.

Josh was called again. "Shelly is being life-flighted to a yet-to-be-determined hospital."

He pulled into a gas station to pray and await further instruction.

My first recollection was being in the air. I recognized I was lying on my back, under medical care, and in a helicopter. I realized something serious had happened, but quickly slipped back into unconsciousness. I came to in a hospital bed with a nurse and two doctors nearby. When asked to state my name, birth date, and where I had been earlier that night, I did so without hesitation. I did not recognize the significance of my ability to remember and speak coherently.

Shortly after, my pastor, his wife, my friend Angie (one of the nurses who administered chest compressions), and my husband Josh arrived.

"Shelly, can you name these people?" a doctor asked.

I did so without hesitation. The doctors were amazed. One doctor declared, "This is nothing short of a miracle!"

I had not expected death to interrupt my camp plans, but God was not surprised. He had orchestrated every detail. He put the right people at the right place at the right time. What could have been a tragedy became a miracle.

Three days later, surgeons implanted a pacemaker/defibrillator in my chest to ensure my heart would never again fail to send the electrical impulse needed to prompt my heart to beat.

The reason I had died was never discovered, but the reason I live is to give God glory.

"I will praise *thee*, O LORD, with my whole heart; I will shew forth all thy marvellous works" (Psalm 9:1).

Bedtime Prayers

As told by Barbara Williams

Six-year-old Judah was devastated. He sobbed, "Mom! Sister Shirley has cancer. She's going to die. She's my favorite Sunday school teacher. She can't die."

Barb Williams sighed. She knew about the doctor's diagnosis and had been dreading the day her son found out. For two years Sister Shirley had been battling cancer. After two surgeries, the doctors had shaken their heads. "It's stage 4. We've done all we can for you. You do not have long to live."

After Judah learned the sad news, every night at bedtime as he knelt with his mother and brother, he reminded them, "Pray that God will heal Sister Shirley."

Night after night they prayed. Sister Shirley's days were numbered. Death was stalking her. She was terminally ill.

Judah was kneeling on the top bunk the night he heard a firm, strong voice in his mind. "It's done. She's healed." Immediately, he stopped praying. He knew God had spoken to him.

He leaned over the top rail. "Mom! Mom, it's done. Sister Shirley is healed. God just told me."

Sister Williams hit the pause button on her prayer. Her eyes bugged. She smiled faintly. "Okay, Son. Since she's healed, let's start praising God."

Judah raised his hands. Over and over he shouted, "Thank You, Jesus, for healing Sister Shirley." After a few minutes, he said, "Now, Mom, you've got to call her and tell her she is healed. Call her right now."

His mother hesitated. "I will call her, Judah, but it's late. She's in bed. I will call her first thing in the morning."

"Promise, Mom?"

"I promise, Judah. I will call her first thing in the morning."

The next morning, she kept her promise. "Sister Shirley, Judah has been praying for you. Last night he told me to call and tell you that God had told him that it is done. You are healed."

Sister Shirley calmly replied, "That's so sweet. But I'm at peace with going to Heaven. If it is God's time to take me, I'm okay with it. Tell Judah thank you for praying for me."

After that, every bedtime prayer at the Williams's house was a praise break. Judah, his brother, and his mother continued to thank God for healing Judah's favorite Sunday school teacher.

The next week Sister Shirley went the doctor for a PET scan. A few days later, the boys were in the garage playing wall ball. His mother ran into the garage, sobbing and shouting, "Judah! Judah! Sister Shirley called. She went to the doctor. She does not have cancer. She is healed!"

Judah nodded. "I know, Mom." Without another word, he threw the ball. He was not surprised. He had a game to win.

"Speak, LORD; for thy servant heareth" (I Samuel 3:9).

Called from the Womb

Submitted by Corinne Nickerson

In 1950 a baby boy was born in Sussex, New Brunswick, Canada. His birth was the answer to Henry and Alena Nickerson's prayers. Many times they had asked God for a son to preach the gospel. But little John's birth was also a rollercoaster of emotions—extreme highs and lows.

It was a difficult birth. The baby's lungs and heart were damaged. In addition, baby Nickerson was born with "infantile paralysis," and his little body was covered with weeping eczema.

The doctor said, "I am sorry, Mr. and Mrs. Nickerson, but your baby will not live."

The Nickersons took their son home, trusting God. Because of the paralysis, John could not eat. Because of the eczema oozing, he suffered constantly and could not be dressed. Every day, every hour was heart-breaking struggle for Henry and Alena and pure torture for their baby.

A few weeks after John's birth, Pastor Allison Post and Missionary Eugene Garrett from the Philippines were directed to the Nickersons' home. Pastor Post knew about their baby, but the missionary did not.

When they entered the house, Missionary Garrett asked, "Who has a sick baby?"

Alena placed her baby in the missionary's arms. He prayed and spoke healing over the suffering baby. He prophesied, "This child will live and preach the gospel in foreign lands." Immediately, the eczema dried up. Gradually, the paralysis improved until John could eat.

Growing up, John enjoyed a healthy, normal childhood. Often, his mother told him about his healing, but never about the prophecy. She determined that his call to the ministry must come from God, not because of her influence.

Only when thirty-two year old John headed for the mission field of Nigeria did she tell him about Missionary Garrett's prophecy. In Africa John reached hundreds of ministers with the truth of Jesus' name baptism.

The gift of healing and the gift of prophecy set John Nickerson on the path God had chosen for him even from the womb.

"Before I formed thee in the belly I knew thee; and before thou camest forth out of the womb I sanctified thee, *and* I ordained thee a prophet unto the nations" (Jeremiah 1:5).

Delayed for a Reason

By Krisann Durnford

Divine healing comes in different ways. Sometimes instantly. Sometimes progressively.

In 1990, I injured my left shoulder. After months of favoring it, all seemed well. Approximately three years later, I re-injured it. What a hassle that injury created! Pain, immobility, and doctor bills plagued me daily. I was a young, energetic adult. This speed bump was frustrating. I was the church pianist. Imagine playing the piano with a screaming shoulder. Simple tasks such as dressing and personal hygiene were nearly impossible without aid.

After tests, I was diagnosed with a frayed nerve directly behind my shoulder blade. The doctor recommended a mix of physical therapy and specific rest periods in a sling. Frayed nerves heal extremely slow (different from "get on your nerves"). Nerves grow back approximately one inch per month, and I had three to five inches of damage.

I prayed, "Lord, I need healing now." My family prayed, "Lord, now." My church family prayed, "Now." Yet, the struggle continued. During that season, the Lord allowed me to witness to an evangelical family. Each weekend the lady and I spent time together studying the Bible, playing with her two youngsters, and shopping. Her husband worked second shift for a family member, and we often had Bible study until his shift was over. They were also praying for my shoulder to heal.

As I wondered why I was not healed, the seeds of the Word were taking root. The husband was a bit skeptical. He asked, "If God is a healer, why aren't you healed?" I did not have an answer.

The seeds germinated. A few weeks after we began the Bible study, my friend called, "Krisann, I just received the Holy Ghost!" Within a short time, she was baptized in Jesus' name. The Lord talked to her about living a separated life. Her husband struggled to accept her conversion. "Why would God bring this division into my family?" We prayed constantly for him . . . and for me.

Deep inside him was a hunger for God. As only Jesus can, He put people and situations in place that this man could not deny. The family business hired a new employee—a Christian who happened to be one of my friends. She intrigued him. Not only did she believe in repentance, baptism in Jesus' name, and the infilling of the Holy Ghost, but she also believed in healing. He was caught off guard, especially when she testified to him about a recent spinal healing.

How exciting to see God working! He was using my affliction to touch others. Still I questioned: "Why am I not healed?"

All the while I was praying, "Now," God was whispering, "Later."

One mid-week service, as I attempted to play, "Look What the Lord Has Done," the enemy sat on my throbbing shoulder and whispered, "Listen to what you are playing. Hear what they are singing: 'He healed my body.' What has God done about your healing? Aren't you a shameful fake! A hypocrite, claiming that He heals when you aren't healed."

Something inside me spoke to that voice, "God is my healer, no matter what I see!"

Immediately, I felt a jolt of electricity flow from the top of my head and down my back. It felt as if God were stitching my back together. I knew I was healed. I jumped from the piano bench and threw both arms in the air. I burst out of the sanctuary, running, shouting. I danced around the building, praising my Lord. I was healed. Later had become now.

My friend's husband could not deny the miracle. A few months later, he was baptized in Jesus' name and filled with the

Holy Ghost. My delayed healing had been to bring the best healing—healing of the soul.

"My soul, wait thou only upon God; for my expectation is from him" (Psalm 62:5).

Ears to Hear

By Susan Bickford

In 1999, my oldest son began having problems with the vision and hearing on his left side. He had already overcome a rough start in life with God's help and many miracles. He was born six weeks early, weighing less than four pounds. It would take an entire book to describe all the miracles associated with his birth. When the problems with his vision and hearing began, we saw it as just another obstacle to overcome through prayer.

Fear reared its ugly head one day in the office of an Ear, Nose and Throat specialist. Eight-year-old Brandon had already had an MRI of his brain, which showed no brain tumor. We had breathed a sigh of relief. But this new doctor put Brandon's head under a special microscope.

"Look here, Mrs. Bickford," he said. I looked and gasped as I saw what lurked inside my son's left ear.

The doctor looked at me sympathetically. "That is a cholesteatoma," he explained. He handed me a brochure and left the room.

I sat there stunned, trying to absorb what had happened. When I read the brochure later, I found out that the cholesteatoma was not cancerous. That was the good news. The bad news? If left untreated, cholesteatoma could damage the eardrum, the bones in the ear, the nerves of the face, and possibly grow into the brain. The only available treatment was surgery to remove it, which almost always resulted in deafness in that ear, and usually nerve damage, which often also caused lifelong, debilitating vertigo. This was not the rosy life I had envisioned for my son!

I have been told that you should always seek a second opinion before any surgery, so our next stop was with a new pediatrician. She looked in Brandon's ear and confirmed the presence of the cholesteatoma. She wanted to refer him to a surgeon, after a visit to the audiologist. The audiologist put a small probe in his ear, which showed a large picture of his ear on a screen. The cholesteatoma looked even more frightening than it had under the microscope. After testing his hearing, she determined that he was already almost deaf in that ear. An appointment was made for a consult with a surgeon.

During this time, I refused to dwell on what might happen, but tried daily to trust God and give Him my fears. We told our pastor about the situation. Many people prayed. A couple of weeks later on a Sunday night, our pastor called Brandon to be prayed for. He anointed him with oil and said a simple prayer. I did not feel any goosebumps or other indication that God was working. Later, I found out that two other churches had special prayer for him that same night.

When we returned home, I got my first inkling of the miracle when Brandon asked, "What's that noise?" He was hearing the traffic on the highway two blocks from our house. While it was so common to me that I had tuned it out, he had never heard it.

A few days later, the surgeon peered into his ear. "Why are you here?" he asked. "There's nothing in this child's ear."

I explained that the cholesteatoma had been documented by two doctors and an audiologist. He refused to believe me. "Why, that would be like someone's legs getting cut off on Wednesday and growing back by Sunday!"

I smiled and said, "Stranger things have happened. Praise God!"

To this day, Brandon has never had another ear infection or hearing problem.

"He that hath ears to hear, let him hear" (Matthew 11:15).

For Sale: One Slightly Used Hospital Bed

Submitted by Charlotte Cotner

I was six years old when Ila Parks knocked on our door. "Lucille, may I take your children to Sunday school?"

Mother hesitated. "Charlotte is old enough. She may go, but the other children are too young."

After that Ila Parks faithfully picked me up for Sunday school at the United Pentecostal Church in Muskogee, Oklahoma. After several months, Mother allowed my siblings to attend.

Not long after, Mother gave birth to twins, making a total of eight children in our family.

One day Sister Parks offered, "Lucille, I would like to come on Sunday morning and help you get the children ready for church so you can go, too."

Sunday after Sunday, this sweet saint of God came early to help Mother. Before long she started picking us up for night services. When I was nine years old, Mother was baptized and received the gift of the Holy Ghost. A year later, I received the Holy Ghost.

About two years after that, Mother was stricken with rheumatoid arthritis. She was so disabled that she could not fix her hair and, at times, could not feed herself. My loving mother watched in physical and emotional agony as I, the oldest child, did her tasks—cooking, laundry, and childcare. My hardworking dad labored from sunup to sundown to keep food on the table and the bills paid. Usually children long for Saturdays, their day of play. But, at our house, Saturday was wash day. My younger sisters and I struggled to push bed sheets, towels, jeans, shirts, dresses and dozens of other items through the wringer on our gasoline-powered washer. We stretched to hang the wash on the outdoor clothesline. It was an all-day job.

One day Dad took Mother to a specialist in Oklahoma City. After three days of testing, the doctor said, "Take her home, Mr. Boswell. Get a wheelchair and a hospital bed. I am sorry, but there is nothing I can do for her. Give her aspirin and cod liver oil to help with the discomfort."

Our family was devastated. The doctor's words sealed our family's new norm, which was not normal at all. Dad was not a Christian, but he believed in prayer and appreciated our pastor Bill Shirel and his wife faithfully coming to pray for Mother.

One day Pastor Shirel asked Mother, "Do you think you can make it to church?"

Mother nodded. "I would like to try."

Pastor Shirel took the back seat out of the church van and, in its place, put an overstuffed chair, a much more comfortable ride. I could tell by the look on Mother's face that she was in agony, but she was determined to go to church. Pastor Shirel moved the chair to the back of the church for Mother.

During the service, he asked her to come up for prayer. He could have gone to her, but he felt led of God to challenge her to put her faith into action. With a look of anguish and a lady on each side, she slowly made her way to the front. After prayer, she shuffled back to her seat. No visible change.

But three days later, she was up doing all the housework, laundry, and cooking and taking care of eight children. Our new norm returned to normal.

From the time my thirty-eight-year-old mother was healed until she died at sixty-seven, she never again had any kind of arthritis. She made up her slightly used hospital bed and sold it.

"Jesus Christ maketh thee whole: arise, and make thy bed" (Acts 9:34).

God's Miracle Package

Submitted by Marney Turpin

How can a person be ecstatic with joy and paralyzed with fear at the same time? My wife and I found out August 30, 1996, the day our son Dustin Ray was born.

The doctor's words drove a sword through our souls. "Your son has spina bifida and hydrocephalus."

These terms were foreign to us, but we soon learned more than we ever wanted to know. Spina bifida damages the nerves in the spine and affects their formation. The doctors could see spinal fluid through a hole at the lower end of Dustin's spine. Spina bifida can result in paralysis, depending on how damaged the nerves are. Hydrocephalus is an accumulation of cerebrospinal fluid (CSF) in the brain. It causes increased pressure inside the skull and is seen in babies as a rapid increase in head size. Other symptoms could include vomiting, sleepiness, seizures, and downward pointing of the eyes.

The doctor continued, "We are rushing your baby to Cooks Children's Hospital in Fort Worth. Depending on how severe the nerve damage is, he may be paralyzed. These conditions, no doubt, will shorten his life expectancy."

Our hearts were crushed, but our faith was strong as we entered the valley of affliction.

The cycle of treatment began. Our little boy was put in a full body cast to straighten his legs. Surgeons inserted a shunt in his skull to relieve the pressure. This led to several surgeries when the shunt plugged up and caused severe headaches. Later the drain tube came loose from the shunt, and the doctors discovered that his ventricles were normal. They did not reconnect the shunt. This was a definite answer to prayer. A miracle. No more shunt.

In addition, Dustin had a condition known as Chiari malformation. The brain tissue extended into his spinal canal. This happens when part of the skull is abnormally small or misshapen, pressing on the brain and forcing it downward. Doctors said our son had suffered brain damage and would not be able to read. Continually, we were on our knees—at times pleading, at times praising, while trusting God for another miracle.

At times it seemed like the bad news would never end. We discovered our son also had scoliosis of the spine. The medical team fused every disk in his back and inserted a rod with screws. He came out of the surgery and never took one pain pill. God allowed him to go through the process but eliminated the pain. Another miracle.

Years passed. We witnessed miracle after miracle. Dustin graduated from high school with excellent reading scores. He is wheelchair bound, but he is not paralyzed. He lives a normal life, reading the Bible without any problem as he studies and preaches the Word of God. God uses him mightily. Many people have received the Holy Ghost under our son's ministry as he travels and conducts revivals.

Dustin Ray Turpin is truly God's miracle package.

"The LORD hath done great things for us; *whereof* we are glad" (Psalm 126:3).

Harper's Heart

By Melissa Pachucki

On February 12, 2018, our perfect baby girl, Harper Pachucki, was born at 8:46 PM. We were instantly in love, but, as first-time parents, we were also instantly scared. The first week was a bit bumpy as we were in and out of the hospital for jaundice treatment.

However, by the second week, everything settled down, and we started adjusting to being a family of three.

At Harper's two-month well-child checkup, the pediatrician heard abnormalities in her heart. She referred us to a cardiologist at OU Children's Hospital. Three weeks later, we took our baby in for an echocardiogram. She smiled and cooed throughout the forty-five-minute test. I thought they would find a basic heart murmur that was so common in newborn babies.

The technician concluded the test and excused herself from the room. When she returned, the head of pediatric cardiology at the Children's Hospital followed her. My heart sank.

He told us that Harper had two murmurs that were typical like we suspected, but there was more. He explained that she also had a congenital heart defect called pulmonary stenosis, which was far less common. Essentially, her pulmonary valve was too thick and not passing enough blood to her lungs. He said that it was natural that we were surprised by the diagnosis since we had not suspected she was sick. With this condition we would never see symptoms until it was incredibly severe. He assured us that he would not let her get that far, but we should prepare ourselves for her surgical options. Our next step was a heart cath to expand the pulmonary valve. However, he noted that there were many risks with the procedure, and it could create other issues. He went on to say that we needed to be fully aware that it was extremely likely that Harper would have to have a valve replacement, which is an open-heart surgery. He was clear that she would need a cardiologist throughout her life, and perhaps valve replacements multiple times as she aged. They would watch and monitor her until she reached six months. At that time, we would decide what course of action to take.

He delivered this news in a matter of ten minutes and sent us on our way. I called my mother on the way home and cried the entire forty-five-minute drive. Everything felt out of my control, and all I could do was pray.

Every night before bed, we laid our hands on Harper's chest and asked God to heal her heart. We took her for prayer at church. We asked friends, family, and church family to pray for a complete healing. Every time I imagined a life of repeated surgeries, I prayed. At her four-month appointment, they ran tests and described the same scenarios. We continued to pray.

On Thursday, September 13, we went back for Harper's cardiology follow up. She underwent multiple tests and exams. They moved us from room to room, advising that they needed to run "just one more test." After repeated nurses, technicians, and doctors had examined Harper, the first cardiologist came in.

He asked us a few questions on how she was functioning, then he described her test results. The holes in her heart were completely closed. There was no sign of them. Her defect was so "trivial" that it had no effect on her whatsoever. Her valve was working normally. Her lungs were receiving plenty of blood. Surgery was no longer necessary. He smiled and said he had no concerns for her anymore. We were to treat her like a child without a heart defect because she was functioning like a child without a heart defect. We openly wept tears of joy in that clinic room as all the stress and fear disappeared.

At her twelve-month check-up, we updated Harper's pediatrician on the status of her condition. Her response was "Wow, that's amazing!" We agreed. We understood that this was never a life-or-death situation, and even that others endure far more difficult experiences. That is why it was so amazing to me. God heard the prayers of a very scared, first-time mom and dad. He saw our precious baby girl. He saw the heart that He had created and chose to strengthen our faith and prove His miraculous power. Our God is good. He hears our prayers!

"A new heart also will I give you" (Ezekiel 36:26).

Her Glory Restored (Part 1)

Submitted by Marsha Jarrell

Ava, a beautiful little girl, was born in 2015 in Perryton, Texas. She was perfect. But as she grew, her baby hair started falling out, and no hair replaced it. Before she was a year old, she was totally bald. No hair on her head. No eyebrows. No eyelashes. It was obvious that something was wrong.

Her family took her to a specialist. She was diagnosed with alopecia areata, an autoimmune disease that causes total hair loss.

The specialist told the family, "I'm sorry. There is no cure for this disease. I cannot give you any hope that Ava will ever have hair."

The family was devastated, especially her grandmother, who knew that a woman's hair is her glory. The thought of her precious granddaughter going through life bald crushed her. She related the doctor's report to her church family. Every time she brought Ava to church, she had her anointed and prayed for. When Ava was not with her, she continued to request prayer for her sweet granddaughter.

The church prayed and prayed and prayed for several months. On April 1, 2018, when little Ava was about three years old, the spirit of intercession fell on the saints during a church service. They united and prayed in one accord for Ava's healing. As they prayed, a prophetic word went forth: "You have asked. I have heard. Now watch Me work!"

The prayers of the saints transformed into praise. "Thank You, Jesus, for giving Ava hair!" "Praise God for healing Ava."

About two weeks later, Ava's grandmother brought her to church. "Look! Everybody, look!" A bit of fuzz covered the top of the toddler's head. Tiny eyelashes were evident. A few months later, Ava's grandmother braided the hair on top of her head.

Every time Ava's grandmother brings her to church, the saints watch as God restores Ava's glory.

At the time this manuscript was submitted for designing, Ava's hair was long enough to be woven into two cute pigtails.

"But the very hairs of your head are all numbered" (Matthew 10:30).

Her Glory Restored (Part 2)

Submitted by Meleah Walker

Author's note. *At Passing the Torch 2019 conference in Pueblo, Colorado, I was asked to share a miracle of my choice from the ones I was compiling for this book. I chose "Her Glory Restored," the previous chapter. At the beginning of the Friday evening service, I read Ava's story and had pictures of her before and after her miracle projected on the screen. One showed little Ava totally bald and the other showed her with dark brown hair. As one unit, the congregation stood, raised their hands, and sent a glory cloud of praise to Heaven.*

Brother Douglas Walker from Yucaipa, California, was the evening speaker. It was the only service of the conference he was able to attend. Near the end of his sermon, he asked, "Where is Sister Westberg?" Several people pointed my direction, and I raised my hand.

He came across the sanctuary and stood in the row in front of me, facing me. He said, "Sister Westberg, I had never heard of alopecia areata until last month when my daughter was diagnosed with it. I am not okay with that!"

I responded, "We are not okay with it, either."

He handed me a handkerchief. "I want to you to pray over this for me to take home to my little girl."

As I raised that handkerchief up to God, a spirit of intercession swept the congregation. The saints' powerful prayers bombarded Heaven.

That weekend three ladies expressed appreciation for that miracle story. They, too, had alopecia areata, and Ava's story had restored their faith.

The following is the continuation of that story, when a heartbroken preacher from California, a discouraged pastor's wife from Arkansas, a saint from Pueblo and an unsaved lady heard the story of a little girl in the panhandle of Texas. All the pieces fell together . . . the right story, the right service, the right people. God's ways are perfect.

Avi Walker's miracle

I sat in my home in Yucaipa, California, listening to the Friday evening service at PTT-19 on Holy Ghost Radio. *What! Did I hear that right? Did Sister Westberg say that little girl had alopecia areata? She did!*

I immediately texted my husband Douglas, who was sitting on the platform in Pueblo, Colorado. That is what Avi has.

In response he snapped a picture of the screen showing a totally bald toddler. He texted it to me. That is when it hit me how serious our Avi's condition was.

In July eleven-year-old Avi had shown me four bald spots on her head. I thought, *Oh my, this can't be good.* But we were busy traveling and enjoying life. When I mentioned it to a friend, her shocked reaction spurred me into making an appointment with a pediatrician.

September 19, 2019, the pediatrician diagnosed her with alopecia areata. We had never heard of such a condition. We had no idea that it was possible for a female to lose all her hair, except as a side effect of chemo. The doctor did not give us any details, and I didn't even know the right questions to ask. She referred us to a dermatologist, and, at the pediatrician's insistence, the dermatologist saw us ten days later.

By this time Avi had eleven bald spots on her head.

Then came that Friday night, October 4, 2019, when I received the screen shot text of little Ava's bald head. My husband brought home the handkerchief that the congregation at PTT had prayed over, and Avi placed it under her pillow.

Right after the conference, at our second visit, the dermatologist told us, "There is no cure for alopecia aerata. Your daughter will continue to lose her hair and eventually be bald. I recommend you purchase a wig and seek counseling to help you through this tragedy. I can put you in touch with a support group."

She went on to share about a girl she had "treated" who was now bald and wearing a wig. Encouraging words? Not!

I was polite to her, but every instinct in me rejected her words. I determined to close every pore of my being to block any seed of negativity. As we left the doctor's office, I proclaimed to Avi, "God is our healer. We will trust Him!" Sometimes those words flow easily, but get stuck in the daily grind of life.

Early every morning I approached the throne of God. "Why? Why, God, would you allow a little girl, whom we have raised to believe according to Scripture that her hair is her glory, to lose her hair?" I wanted a reason. I begged for a reason.

We anointed Avi's head. We prayed. We cried. We believed. We listened repeatedly to the recording of Ava's miracle as told that night at Passing the Torch. Often in the middle of an activity, my husband would pick up the phone and call a friend. Multiple times I heard him asking people around the country to pray for our baby girl.

By October 31, Avi had seventeen bald spots.

Sometimes God performs immediate miracles. Sometimes healing is a process, and other times, God leads us to the sources that can help us.

We went to see a family medicine physician who is certified in Integrative Holistic Medicine (holistic, but science-based). She grabbed Avi's hands and looked into her eyes. "Avi, there is a cure. I believe something isn't right in your gut. Let's start with a gluten- and dairy-free diet."

She believed that Avi's system could not process gluten, causing her to become allergic to her hair. This happens often in autoimmune diseases.

We went home and changed Avi's diet drastically.

She was scheduled to have steroids injected into her scalp in early December. When we visited the dermatologist for this procedure, she was shocked. In four weeks Avi's hair had started growing back. The injections were not needed because her hair was growing faster than it would have with an injection. She noted that the hair would grow back white first, then change to the natural color. Avi's hair's natural color was already being restored.

Avi had been on a gluten-free diet for six months by the end of May 2020. She was referred to a gastroenterologist for more extensive testing, including an endoscopy. The doctor asked us to slowly incorporate gluten back into her diet before the endoscopy for accurate results. After the tests, the doctor compared endoscopy and blood-work panel with the one taken in November.

"I find nothing irregular!" the doctor reported.

As of this writing, a little over a year from the time our daughter was diagnosed with alopecia areata, she is completely healed. She eats whatever she wants. Her hair has grown back. She has zero bald spots.

To God be the glory for restoring our baby girl her glory!

"To the end that *my* glory may sing praise to thee, and not be silent. O LORD my God, I will give thanks unto thee for ever" (Psalm 30:12).

Hidden Scars

Submitted by Neva (Scott) Limones

In 1968 while my family was on the mission field in Ecuador, we received a distressing message that my grandmother, Ethel Jordan, had been rushed to the hospital with a possible heart attack. We did what we could, the best thing anyone can do in an emergency. We prayed.

Later we learned that, in the Emergency Room, they had checked her and found absolutely nothing wrong. They had sent her home. Grandmother declared that the Lord had healed her! But she had no proof.

In March 1982 my seventy-three-year-old grandmother had to have a tumor removed from her breast. After the surgery, I was in the room with her when the doctor came in.

"Your past heart surgery was the finest I have ever seen," he said. "On the X-ray I noticed a scar on your heart. I could tell you had a mitral valve collapse. That usually kills a person before surgery can be performed. It is an extremely difficult surgery to perform. But the stitches were perfect. Apparently, you had a first-rate surgeon."

My grandmother answered, "But I have no scars from a previous surgery."

The doctor mentally reviewed what he had seen of her chest before the mastectomy. Shocked, he acknowledged, "That is true." No outward scars. Hidden scars left by internal stitches. He shook his head. "Only the Great Physician could have done it!"

The next morning the therapist came to start treatment. Grandmother was fixing her hair. (She was not vain, but always wanted to look her best.)

His mouth fell open. He tossed her a ball and said, "It doesn't look like you need this. You shouldn't even be able to move your arm."

The Great Physician had performed major surgery without a scalpel or needle. Stitched the damaged mitral valve and left hidden scars to be revealed some fourteen years later.

"[I will] make you a new heart and a new spirit, for why will ye die?" (Ezekiel 18:31).

Jesus, My Keeper

Submitted by Shirley Engelhardt

The year was 2009. The year we celebrated our fortieth wedding anniversary. The year that brought a deep trial that affected our family and zeroed on me.

One fine April day after I completed my weekly house cleaning, fatigue overwhelmed me. I dismissed it as a chance occurrence.

In early May, after our annual ladies' retreat, while loading the car I felt chilled. Again, I dismissed it. By Friday, I was chilling and had fever. The fever broke on Monday but returned almost daily. My doctor diagnosed it as a sinus infection and ordered an antibiotic. When I went off the antibiotic, the fever returned. When I didn't take Tylenol, my fever spiked dangerously. Twice I had near convulsions.

While teaching at kid's camp, I became extremely ill. My doctor sent me to an infectious disease specialist who ordered a picc line inserted in my upper arm and put me on antibiotics. I had endocarditis (a blood infection in the inner lining of the heart chambers and valves). For two months antibiotics fed into my system 24/7. The condition persisted. My doctor recommended open-heart surgery.

Ministering brethren prayed that I would be spared the surgery. However, I felt this was the path God had chosen for me. I had to trust Him in a way I had never imagined. Every step was taken with His directive. Choices were made prayerfully and carefully.

We could not afford insurance. Bills soared. Medical bills mounted to $150,000. We were in danger of losing our home. We clung to God's promises.

Overwhelmed? Yes. Forsaken? Never.

The day for my surgery approached. The Lord set in order the right surgeon, the right hospital, and our finances. One of the medical staff took us to the finance office. By the end of the day, all bills were covered. It would have cost us thousands of dollars personally had we not been given financial aid. We praise the Lord for His ever-watchful care for us.

On October 6, 2009, I received a mechanical heart valve to replace my mitral valve that the infection was destroying. After a month, the pic line was removed.

My healing was not instantaneous, but nevertheless real. As they said it might, it took me five years to return to my normal routine. But it happened.

Fast forward to September 2015. Another crisis.

In early September, I was diagnosed with stage 3 colon cancer. My one remaining ovary was filled with cysts. Cancer? It sounded like a death sentence. Another surgery? Overwhelming! But I had no options. I trusted God to order my steps.

Test after test after test after test. I was exhausted. Then the surgery. Three days later I was out of the hospital. They had removed a 3mm mass of cancer and three lymph nodes.

I will never forget "Black Tuesday." I was hit by the most dangerous moment and side effect possible. I was rushed to the hospital by ambulance and given blood transfusions. Drifting in and out of consciousness, I heard the nurses say, "She is hemorrhaging. We can't waste any time getting her to surgery."

I whispered, "Jesus, You are my keeper."

After surgery, the surgeon recommended chemotherapy. Chemo? I could not wrap my mind around this possibility.

In November, I had a follow-up visit with the surgeon. He urged me to take chemotherapy and recommended an oncologist, whom I went to see. I left his office with a complete portfolio of the recommended treatment. My husband and I studied the treatment and side effects. Then we took it all to Jesus, laid it at His feet, and trusted that He was in control.

The decision was made. No chemo. Instead, I found alternatives to help prevent "possible recurrence of cancer." The Lord led me to sources that helped me stay healthy through my diet. Today, I am clean and clear of any cancer. I keep my special diet at the directive of the Lord.

As before, my healing was not instantaneous, but nevertheless real.

Through this journey I have learned to walk with Jesus at a much deeper level. I know without a doubt that Jesus is my keeper.

"Thou shalt keep them, O LORD, thou shalt preserve them from this generation for ever" (Psalm 12:7).

Jesus' Smile

Submitted by Kathy McAuley

In the early 1960s in Tulsa, Oklahoma, four-year-old Teri was hospitalized with meningitis. Six other children were in Hillcrest Hospital at the same time with the same disease. All were in grave condition.

Little Teri was in a coma. The doctors gave the family no hope for her recovery. But on the slim chance that she did survive, they said that she would be mentally impaired and basically in a vegetative state.

Teri's parents, Lester and Wilma Mullis, were expecting their fifth child. Due to Wilma's pregnancy, she was not allowed to see her daughter. When the doctors told the parents that there was nothing more they could do, Wilma insisted she was going to see her little girl.

In the meantime, the family prayed.

At the hospital, the distraught mother put on a gown and mask. When she looked in the window of Teri's isolation room, she saw that the IV had been disconnected. A nurse stood beside the bed. A sheet was pulled over her little girl. Wilma's heart fell into her stomach. She wailed, "My baby girl is dead!"

Another nurse touched her shoulder. "Oh, no! Come in and see!"

When Wilma walked into the room, Teri was patting her foot as she sang, "Jesus loves me this I know." Wilma's tears collided with her smile. She approached the bed. Teri's radiant face lit up the room.

The little girl pointed at her mother's mask. "Mama, take that thing off!"

Wilma started to tell her she could not, but Teri continued, "I want to see if your smile looks like Jesus' smile."

Wilma eyes popped. "Teri, are you telling me that you saw Jesus?"

"Yes. He came into my room and put His hand on my head. He said, 'Teri, I'm Jesus. I'm healing you, and you can go home and play with your sisters. You will never be sick like this again.'" Then she described His garment.

Teri survived by the hand of Jesus! She had no permanent signs of ever being sick. Sadly, the six other children with meningitis who were in the hospital at that time died. The doctor said that it was nothing they had done that had healed Teri. They had treated all seven of the children the same.

Wilma remembers the doctor pointing up and saying, "This was definitely from a Higher Power."

Through the years, when faced with grave situations, Teri's family has always looked to her miraculous healing for encouragement and faith, knowing God does hear and answer prayer.

"God be merciful unto us, and bless us; *and* cause his face to shine upon us" (Psalm 67:1).

Migraines Be Gone!

Submitted by Jan Vaughan

It started as a typical May day in Clinton, Oklahoma. My husband Larry was working out of town. Brenda and Brook, our daughters, climbed into our Explorer. My five-day-a-week plan was: (1) take the girls to school, then (2) go to my job at the florist. On this typical day, things did not go as I had planned. That day altered my life for twenty-two years.

As we neared town, I heard that still, small voice urge, "Put on your seat belts." I did not listen. My mind was on a thousand other things.

As we came into town, a young man ran a stop sign. The impact hit the front of our Explorer, turned it around, and hit the back. I hit my head on the rearview mirror and cracked the windshield. We skidded to a stop on the bank parking lot, and he landed across the street. Miraculously, the girls were not hurt.

The bank called the fire chief, who was not far away. The code went out to all fire department volunteers informing them that there had been an accident involving a volunteer's family. (Larry was that volunteer fireman.) The entire fire department showed up—husbands and wives.

I was transported to the hospital. The wives stayed with me, taking care of the girls.

The medical team agreed, "Of course, your head hurts after the blow you suffered. In time it will get better. Meanwhile, take these pain pills."

I was sent home.

That was the beginning of my life with migraines. At times the pain was so severe that I would pass out. My husband, a friend, or whoever was available would take me to the hospital for a shot or two. One night at church, the pain was so intense that I started to leave, but only got as far as the back pew where I collapsed. No one could wake me up. Another ER visit.

We lived several miles out in the country. When Larry was out of town on business, it was not safe for the girls and I to stay alone. A kind couple in the church opened their home to us. We spent many nights with them.

During these years, I struggled to maintain a normal life, working a full-time job, participating in church camps, and caring for my family. Often I would tell my coworkers, "Sorry. I have lie down." At times when I walked outside, the sunlight pierced my eyes and started my head throbbing. I spend many, many days in bed with the blinds pulled and a pillow over my eyes.

The prescriptions multiplied. I gained weight. My outgoing, life-of-the-party personality faded. I was prayed for many times, but still I suffered. So, after years of living with a pounding headache and nausea, I accepted that this was the way my life would always be.

On what seemed like an ordinary October day, Larry and I helped with a wedding. I did the bride's bouquet, and Larry videoed it. At the reception, I said, "Larry, my head is busting. We have to go. I can't handle being here any longer."

My lifelong friend Veronica Peters walked up. "How are you doing, Jan?"

I placed my palm on my forehead. "Not too good. We are leaving, but I wanted to see the fellowship hall first."

"Colby needs to pray for you," she said. "He has the gift of healing."

Veronica motioned to her son and led me toward him. Colby was aware of my chronic migraines. He gathered a few people around me.

He instructed, "We are not going to ask for Jan's healing. We are going to command the migraines to leave." They prayed. Oh, how they prayed! Their prayers echoed throughout the hall and church. But I felt nothing. No lightning bolt. No electrical shock. No warm fuzzy feeling. Nothing. Everyone returned to celebrating. Larry took me home.

The next morning when I awakened, I swung my feet to the floor. I stood. Something was different. I shook my head. No throbbing. No pain. No headache! All day and the next night, no headache. I did not take any medication. After three pain-free, med-free days, I threw all my medication in the trash. Everyone knows that when you have been on pain prescriptions for years, you don't quit cold turkey. But I did.

That was four years ago at this writing. I have not had one more migraine headache. My husband told Colby, "I've got my Jannie back."

Why didn't God heal the first time I was prayed for? I don't know. I only know that once I suffered migraines, but now they are gone!

"For I will restore health unto thee, and I will heal thee of thy wounds, saith the LORD" (Jeremiah 30:17).

Peace, Be Still

Submitted by Candace Agans

M omma, my right leg hurts. It really hurts," ten-year-old Sara complained.

I figured it was a growing pain since she had grown 7" in the last year. "It will be okay. Just walk it off."

It was January 2019. The following Wednesday, the pain seemed slightly worse. Still convinced it was a growing pain, I gave her Ibuprofen and a heating pad. She stayed in bed on Thursday with the heating pad, taking Ibuprofen every four to six hours. I went to bed exhausted that evening after she finally fell asleep. I was not aware that she woke up and cried for the rest of the night. Early Friday morning she dragged herself to my room and awakened me. She could not put any weight on her right leg.

Fearing the worst, I dressed quickly and carried her to the vehicle. We went straight to her pediatrician's office.

The doctor did not know that Sara's dad, Billyjoe, had a rheumatoid disease that affects his hips and legs. Right away she asked, "What type of rheumatoid diseases run on each side of your families?"

She sent Sara to the hospital for blood work. When it came back positive, I was not surprised.

We were referred to a rheumatologist at Le Bouhner Children's Hospital in Memphis, Tennessee. The blood work was done again, and they ran an MRI. The blood work showed nothing out of the ordinary. The MRI, however, revealed inflammation along her pelvic bone and a tumor at the top of her femur where it connected to the hip bone.

We were told that it was likely a benign osseous tumor. An orthopedic surgeon would remove it. After Sara healed from surgery, she would be fine. There was a slight chance it was osseous lymphoma. They scheduled a repeat MRI in a month to see if the tumor had grown.

It was the longest month of my life. A tsunami of fear swept over me. Winds of doubt battered my faith.

In March they repeated the tests.

When I read the online report, the emotional thunderstorm I had been in escalated into a tornado. I was devastated. My heart dropped. I gasped. I sobbed. The report said my sweet little 10-year-old had osseous lymphoma, an exceedingly rare cancer that begins in the bones instead of the blood. There is an 80-percent survival rate.

Sara's doctor did not call until the following day. I was furious. Why did she leave me waiting that long, knowing that the report was posted on Sara's online account already? She had to have known I was panicking!

She said, "The MRI technician is absolutely sure it is lymphoma. There is no doubt in our minds." She explained that the previous day she had been on the phone with a specialist getting a team of doctors together to come up with a plan. The specialist had been reviewing Sara's results. He wanted to see her first thing on Monday. We were being transferred to St. Jude Children's Hospital. This is the last thing any parent wants to hear.

I was falling apart. Overwhelming sorrow and anger whirled in me. I have never dealt with depression, but, at that moment, I understood what it feels like.

I have always been a person of faith. I have always believed that my God can do anything. I have always been the one that my family and friends came to when they needed someone to pray. At that moment, I was drained. My faith lay face down in the dirt. I wish I could say that I knelt to pray, and my faith was restored immediately. But that's not what happened.

Somehow, I choked out the words to tell my husband what the doctor had said. We started calling. Our plea for prayer went across the nation to friends and family. They shared our shocking news with their churches and everyone who would pray.

When Sara was around, we put on our strong-parent facade so she wouldn't panic. But when I was alone, uncontrollable sobs shattered me. I yelled at God. I begged Him to stop the storm. "God, why this was happening?" I could not understand.

My husband, Sara, and I went to St Jude's on Monday. They walked us through our daily routine, showing us the ins and outs. It is an amazing place, but I would rather see it on a tour than registering my child for treatment. We spent most of the day there.

After they had drawn Sara's blood, they took us to the clinic that would be treating her. We were left waiting in a bleak room. It seemed like an eternity before the doctor came in. *Smiling? Why was he smiling?*

He said, "I have reviewed the results of her blood work and gone over the MRI images. Nothing resembles any kind of cancer. Just to be sure I am reading everything correctly, I am having another doctor review these tests."

We took a deep breath. *Could it be true? Oh, God, could it be true?*

About an hour later, both doctors came in. "No sign of cancer anywhere," they agreed.

Relief flooded my soul. Chill bumps covered my body. My heart danced. Billyjoe and I laughed and cried. At our most frightening moment, God had stepped in. He spoke to our storm, "Peace, be still." Suddenly, there was a great calm.

The results from later tests read: "Osseous lymphoma not likely because osseous lymphoma cannot heal itself without treatment. No sights of rheumatoid disease." Not only was Sara healed of cancer, but God also healed her rheumatoid disease!

Praise report: On January 22, 2020, Sara was officially released from St Jude and Le Bouhner! Oh happy day!

"And [Jesus] arose, and rebuked the wind, and said unto the sea, "Peace, be still. And the wind ceased, and there was a great calm" (Mark 4:39).

Performed in the Womb

Submitted by Neva Limones

Borger, Texas. Ana came to the front for prayer. Her shoulders shook as tears flowed. "Today I went to the doctor. They did an ultrasound." She choked on the next words. "My baby . . . my baby has no . . . has no legs."

We were shocked, but reminded ourselves that with our God nothing was impossible. My husband anointed her with oil in the name of Jesus. The church prayed.

After service was dismissed, Ana remained at the altar weeping. I left the organ to sit beside her. Compassion overwhelmed me. As Ana's former Sunday school teacher, I knew her story. As her pastor's wife, I wept with her. As a mother, I felt her pain.

Without thinking, I blurted out, "Don't worry about this. When your baby is born, he will be perfectly fine."

My words comforted her, but they terrified me. *Why did I tell her that? What if God doesn't heal the baby? She trusts me. She'll call me a liar. She will be so hurt.* My faith plummeted, "O God, forgive me for being so presumptuous."

Later, when Ana showed me that ultrasound image, my faith took another dive. The head and trunk of the baby were formed. The arms were evident. But there were no legs.

A few months later, Ana went into labor. When the baby was born, everyone in the labor room gasped. Two arms. Two hands. Ten fingers. Two legs. Two feet. Ten toes. Ana's baby boy was born perfectly whole!

Some seventeen years later, my husband and I had occasion to return to Borger. We were introduced to a husky, healthy high school boy with two legs, two feet, ten toes—Ana's son.

How different life would have been for this lad had God not performed a miracle as he was being formed in his mother's womb.

"Thus saith the LORD, thy redeemer, and he that formed thee from the womb, I *am* the LORD that maketh all *things*" (Isaiah 44:24).

Persistent Prayer and Pain

Submitted by Deanne Little

Our section's twenty-mile March for Missions was marked on the calendar. It was time to get in shape if we were going to cooperate and march with our two teen daughters and the youth of the church we pastored. My husband and I pulled out our bicycles.

In the 1980s Wagoner, Oklahoma, was a safe place. We had no qualms about riding around our neighborhood day or night. No crime. No threats. No danger. But we forgot one thing . . . dogs!

One night as we huffed and puffed and pumped, I heard a threatening growl and felt teeth nipping at my heels. I am not afraid of dogs, normally. But normally they do not nip at my heels. I lost my balance and landed in a ditch on my shoulder. Ooohhh! I screamed as intense pain radiated through my whole body. My husband, Jerry, was immediately at my side. I don't know what happened to the dog! Maybe my scream scared him.

We went for medical help immediately. When they x-rayed my shoulder, I passed out.

The doctor read the X-ray and announced, "No damage." He prescribed a pain pill and sent me home.

The pills ran out. The pain continued. A couple of weeks later, I returned to the doctor. He gave me shock treatments in the area of my shoulder. More intense pain.

We were pastoring a small home missions church. I was the only musician. So, every service I played the piano, sang, and cried. The pain persisted.

What does a Pentecostal do when she is in pain? She prays without ceasing and asks for prayer every chance she gets. For five months at every service, I asked for prayer.

My teenage daughters were so embarrassed. "Not again, Mother! Do you have to go for prayer every service?"

March for Missions time came. My family marched. I sat at home in pain and cried.

Finally, I went to a specialist in Tulsa. He ordered X-rays. His prognosis: "Your collarbone is chipped, and your shoulder is out of socket. It can only be corrected by major surgery. Furthermore, you will have arthritis in that shoulder for the rest of your life." He also did what doctors seldom do. He criticized the first doctor. "Shock treatments were the worst possible treatment for that injury."

The cost of the surgery was estimated to be several thousand dollars. No insurance. No money. What were we to do? Keep praying and asking for prayer.

"Mother! Not again!"

"Yes, girls, again and again until God heals me."

"Mother! Stop making a show of yourself."

"Girls, whatever it takes. I am going to keep asking for prayer until God heals me."

One Sunday night I again went to the front for prayer. My husband anointed me with oil in the powerful name of Jesus. The saints gathered around and prayed. I lost awareness of everything but the presence of God. My husband said that, as I worshipped, I raised and waved the arm that I had not lifted in six months. When the prayer ended, my shoulder was in place. The pain was gone!

The next day I cleaned out my kitchen cabinets. That night I ached all over. I fretted. *The pain is back. I wasn't healed.* But I was healed! I was only sore because I had exercised muscles that had not been used for six months.

At this writing I am eighty years old and do not have, and never have had, arthritis. When God does a job, He does it right.

"Prayer was made without ceasing of the church unto God" (Acts 12:5).

Surprise Visit

Submitted by Merlin Wilson

Benton, Arkansas in 1950. For a week nine-year-old Laman Wilson had suffered a raging fever as pneumonia infiltrated his lungs. His temperature was so high the little boy slept with his eyes open. His father and pastor, Earl Wilson, had strong convictions against seeking medical help—a conviction held by many in his generation. The saints in the church were pressuring Pastor Wilson to take his son to the doctor.

Monday morning the heartbroken dad knelt beside his son's bed. "God, I can't stand to see him suffer anymore. Either take him or heal him."

He went into the living room and waited for the God he trusted to do something. What? He did not know.

In a few minutes a voice from the bedroom said, "Daddy, can I get up?"

His father answered, "If you feel like it."

The boy got up. "Daddy, I'm hungry."

As he sent praises upward, Pastor Wilson fixed Laman something to eat.

Next question. "Daddy, can I go out and play?"

"If you feel like it."

The screen door slammed as the boy ran out the back door.

A few minutes later there was a knock on the door. Pastor Wilson was surprised to see two men in uniform standing there.

"Reverend Wilson, may we come in?"

Laman's dad opened the door wide. "Certainly. Come in."

The first man introduced himself. "I am the sheriff of Saline County. This is my deputy. We understand that you have a sick boy here."

"Yes, sir. He's been mighty sick."

"May we see him?"

"Certainly. He's in the backyard playing."

Surprise, gentlemen. The Great Physician visited the scene before you arrived.

"And immediately he arose, took up the bed, and went forth before them all; insomuch that they were all amazed, and glorified God, saying, We never saw it on this fashion" (Mark 2:12).

The Breath of Life

Submitted by Bobby Jarrell

Tires squealed. A loud thump! Screaming!

What was going on? I jumped to my feet, dropped my wrench and almost knocked over the pan holding the oil draining from my work truck. I ran around the corner of my house and paused a moment to listen. The commotion was coming from the intersection down the street where a crowd had gathered. I raced to join them.

A little boy wearing shorts was laying the street. Totally still. Totally silent. One eye was rolled up in his head, and the other eye looking straight up. He was not breathing.

His mother stood about twenty feet away in shock repeating, "Please somebody help my baby! Please somebody help my baby!"

Another little boy who appeared to be the injured boy's brother was sobbing. I picked the crying child up. "It's going to be okay. It's going to be okay."

Like a CD on a loop, the mother kept repeating, "Please somebody help my baby!"

I put the boy down and almost without thought, I stepped to the injured boy's side and knelt. A man from across the street knelt beside me. I placed my hand lightly on the child's forehead and prayed, "Jesus, if it is his time to go, take him . . . but if not, breathe the breath of life back into him."

I stood up and stepped back onto the sidewalk. I watched while whispering, "In Jesus name. In Jesus name." Slowly, very slowly, the boy's chest rose . . . up . . . down . . up . . down . . up down, up down up down. By the time the ambulance arrived, he was moaning.

I turned to go finish changing the oil in my truck. The man who had knelt beside me held out his hand. I stopped.

"I want to ask you a question."

I nodded. "Okay."

"That boy was not breathing. Right?"

I shook my head. "Right. He was not breathing.

"He was dead."

"Yes, he was dead," I said while my heart sang, "Thank You, Jesus."

I walked back to my truck shuddering under the power of God.

Later I learned the only injury the boy suffered was a broken arm. To God be the glory.

"Not unto us, O LORD, not unto us, but unto thy name give glory" (Psalm 115:1).

The Holy Ghost's Prayer Request

Submitted by Billie Jo Arp

In 1988 while living with my grandparents in Stuart, Oklahoma, I became ill and was prescribed a high dosage of steroids. Later the dosage was lowered to what the doctor called a lifetime dosage for me.

Ten years later I started having problems with my left hip. My doctor ordered a bone density scan of my hip. He showed me the results.

"Look. See how your hip is breaking down? This is from the long-term use of steroids. Eventually you will have to have a hip replacement."

We agreed that I should wait for the surgery until the pain level increased. My damaged hip was uncomfortable at times, but not a hindrance to normal life.

In 1998 I was transferred to Durango, Colorado, where I met and became friend with Teresa. In 2001 I was transferred to Pueblo. To my surprise and delight, Teresa's job also transferred her to Pueblo. We loved the Pueblo church family and pastor.

When my company sent me to Denver for about a month, my hip started giving me excruciating pain. I could barely walk. I made an appointment to see my rheumatologist in Pueblo the next morning.

I called Teresa. "Please pray for me. The pain from my hip is almost unbearable. I am coming back to Pueblo in the morning to see my doctor."

She replied, "Tonight is church. I will request prayer for you."

The next morning when I awoke, I had no pain, but because of my past experiences with pain coming and going, I kept my appointment. The technician took a bone density test and left me in the exam room to wait for the doctor's report. Everyone who has ever sat in a doctor's exam room has experienced the tension—five minutes seems like twenty.

Finally, the doctor came in holding a folder. He grunted at me but did not make eye contact. He walked directly to the corner desk and sat with his back to me on a black-padded, wheeled stool (the kind found in all exam rooms).

I watched as he shuffled the papers and muttered to himself, "I just don't understand. I just don't understand."

After a few minutes of his strange behavior, my patience died. I asked, "What exactly don't you understand?"

He abruptly wheeled around. He raised his voice a few decibels. "How long have you been on Prednisone?"

"For fourteen years. Why?"

"Fourteen years? Don't you understand what happens to people who have only been on this drug for a year or two?"

"Yes, I understand. What are you getting at?"

His demeanor tightened. He raised his voice a few more decibels, barely below a shout. "Look! Look at these pictures! Look at your hip before and now. The before picture shows your hip severely damaged, but this one. . . ." He held up the picture taken that morning. "This one shows a perfect hip. There is nothing wrong with this hip."

Tears flowed down my cheeks. I stood up. "It's okay, doctor. You don't have to understand. I do. I have been praying, and my friends have been praying. God has regrown my hip bone!"

His mouth fell open.

I grabbed my purse. "Thank you, doctor. I have to go."

As soon as I got to my car, I dialed Teresa with shaking fingers. When she answered, I blurted out, "Teresa, you are not going to believe what—"

She interrupted. "Billy Jo, I have something to tell you!"

What could be more important than my miracle? I let her speak first.

"A visiting minister from Tupelo, Mississippi, was at church last night. I didn't get to request prayer for you because the schedule changed. As he was preaching, an amazing thing happened. He stopped and said, 'Church, the Holy Ghost just spoke to me. There is a lady from this church working out of town. She desperately needs our prayers right now.' I knew that was you."

Teresa had not requested prayer for me, but the Holy Ghost had!

My job has transferred me to many places since then, but I continued to have regular checkups including X-rays and bone density scans. As of the last scan in Spokane, Washington, my hip bone is perfect.

"Oh that I might have my request; and that God would grant *me* the thing that I long for!" (Job 6:8).

The Power of the Word

Submitted by Richard Montez

December 29, 2015, was the day I first put on the cap I will wear the rest of my life—my dad's cap. I sat in the hospital room holding our newborn son as my wife Cathy slept, recovering from a difficult labor. How can a father put in words the feeling of holding his child for the first time? Frightened? Proud? Humble?

I examined my son. Ten toes. Ten fingers. Flawless features. Josiah Allen Montez was picture-perfect. God had blessed Cathy and I with His greatest miracle—a baby.

I sat awkwardly holding Josiah when a nurse came in. "I need to take your baby for some routine tests."

My arms felt empty as she carried our son down the hall. I was not worried—not too much anyway. Josiah was perfect, wasn't he?

After about an hour she returned and laid Josiah back in my arms. She said, "Your son passed every test, except one—the hearing test. In a little bit we will try again. Don't worry."

It was just a fluke, I consoled myself. Our son was perfectly healthy. As Cathy and Josiah slept, I planned the future. All the things I would do with my son, the things I would teach him. *How old would he have to be before I could start teaching him to play the keyboard?*

The nurse returned and once again took Josiah to the exam room. This time when she returned, she looked worried. "He still didn't pass the hearing test." She offered me a sliver of hope. "I will be back in about an hour to try again."

She walked out and fear walked in. *What if our son is deaf? What will we do? How will we provide his needs? What kind of life will he have?* The unknowns smothered me. My lungs jerked. My eyes blurred. I had no answers. No solutions. Only questions. *What would the future look like for Josiah?*

I reached for the Bible and opened it to Romans 10:17. I read, "So then faith *cometh* by hearing, and hearing by the word of God." I gently placed the open Bible against my son's tiny ear and prayed. "God, I know that You are in control of all things. Our lives have been founded upon Your Word. I have faith that You are able to heal our son and his hearing will be fine." I continued praying, grasping every promise from God's Word I could remember.

For the third time the nurse took our baby to the exam room. Every minute she was gone seemed like an eternity. I continued to pray softly.

Then she returned smiling. "He passed the hearing test. I don't know what happened between the first time and this time, but he passed the test. His hearing is fine."

My lungs relaxed as she again placed Josiah in my arms. The tears that had blurred my vision now rolled down my face in blessed release. I knew what had happened. God had heard the prayers of this new dad who had faith in His Word. God had sent His word and healed Josiah.

"He sent his word, and healed them" (Psalm 107:20).

The Still, Small Voice

Submitted by Sarah Salas

Twelve-year-old Sarah, her younger sister Anna, and her cousin Andrew were doing their balancing act—walking back and forth on the drainage pipe over the ten-foot-deep drainage ditch behind the girls' house. It was exhilarating. One carefully placed step after another with outstretched arms flapping like chicken wings. Gulps! Gasps! Shrieks! Each time they crossed, they paused a moment to congratulate one another and relish the high of their death-defying stunt. Then back on the pipe for another stroll across the tightrope over Niagara.

Sarah was almost to home base when a strong blast of wind knocked her off balance. She looked down into the stinky, dirty water. The gutter or the dirt-packed bank? It was a no-brainer. She dove for the bank. Crack! She screamed as her elbow popped! Her head whirled. Her stomach heaved. Pain radiated through her body.

Anna and Andrew yelled. "Sarah, are you okay? Sarah, answer me!"

Sarah moaned. "I think I am going to pass out."

Andrew looked at Anna. They looked at Sarah. "Ahhh, it can't be that bad. You just hit your crazy bone. Don't be a crybaby."

Sarah crawled to the top of the bank, favoring her injured arm. She gasped for breath. Each beat of her heart was echoed in her throbbing elbow. The pain was excruciating. She gnashed her teeth, stuffing down the screams. She clutched her elbow close to her body. She would not be a crybaby!

As they walked toward the house, the girls' mother pulled into the driveway. "What's wrong, Sarah?" she called.

Sarah struggled to answer. "I fell off the drainage pipe. I think my elbow is broken."

At the doctor's office, the doctor studied the X-rays. "Sarah has a cracked elbow. She will need to wear a sling for three weeks. After that we will take another X-ray. If it hasn't healed, we will put her arm in a cast."

That night a revival started at Apostolic Faith Tabernacle in Hutchinson, Kansas, where Sarah's dad, Carl Elder, pastored. Sarah sat in her usual pew, supporting her aching arm. She weakly joined the congregation in worship.

Suddenly she heard a still, small voice in her right ear. "If you will run, I'll heal you!"

What? She looked around. *I must be imagining things.*

"If you will run, I will heal you." There it was again—that voice.

She peered over her shoulder, trying not to be too obvious. She shrugged. *I think I am hallucinating because of the pain.*

"If you will run, I will heal you." The voice was louder.

She came out her pew like an apostolic youth on fire and ran toward the pulpit.

When she reached the center of the pulpit, a warm sensation started at the top of her head. It spread down the left side of her neck and body. When it touched her elbow, it felt like hot oil was poured on it. It was not painful, but surprisingly comforting.

Pop! She felt and heard her elbow snap back into place. She pulled off the sling, threw up her arm, praising God and shouting for joy!

After church she told her parents that God had healed her elbow. They rejoiced with her, but said, "Tomorrow we will take you back to the doctor for verification. We need to be sure you are okay without the sling."

As the doctor studied the second X-ray, he smiled. "Young lady, you are very blessed! Your God has done a miracle! Your elbow is healed. You do not need a sling or a cast."

Sarah's amazing God again confirmed Himself to her. Now a married woman with a teen daughter, Sarah rejoices when she remembers the night she obeyed that small voice and God performed a miracle just for her.

"We will obey the voice of the LORD our God, . . . that it may be well with us" (Jeremiah 42:6).

The Unseen Hand

Submitted by Ella Borders

ummer 1947. Greenfield, Illinois. My fifteen-year-old brother John Mohr was thrilled to have a summer job, working for a farmer.

What fun driving a tractor, until the tractor overheated. John hopped off, went to the front, and opened the radiator cap. Definitely not the thing to do. Boiling water erupted like a fountain and scalded him from face to waist.

The farmer came racing across the field. He cringed when he saw John. "Do you want to go to the hospital?"

Grimacing in pain and biting his lips to keep from screaming, John sobbed, "No. Just take me home."

The hour-long trip was a blur of excruciating pain.

As a ten-year-old, I watched the farmer carry John in and lay him on the floor in our family room. His upper body was covered in huge water blisters.

Dad was at work, and we only had one car. Mother took charge. "Ella, ride your bike to the pastors' house and tell them that this is an emergency." With the ugly picture of my brother crying in agony, I pedaled the four blocks to our pastors' house.

No one was home.

"Go up and down the street to the saints' houses. Get everyone you can find to come and pray," Mother ordered.

With tears rolling, my legs pumping, and my heart thumping, I managed to find five or six church ladies at home. They gathered around John and prayed. I mean *prayed*.

"Ella, close the blinds," Mother said. She thought it best to keep inquisitive eyes out. No telling how the story of the prayer meeting would evolve after being spread by the town's gossips.

The prayer warriors wept and travailed. Minutes, maybe even an hour, passed. No one knew how long because we were not watching the clock.

I watched and sobbed as the ladies prayed and John writhed in pain. Then my mouth fell open. One by one the blisters disappeared as an unseen hand moved down John's burned body. His red burned skin returned to its normal color.

John sat up and smiled. "I feel fine."

I don't know how long the intercession lasted, but it ended with a loud Pentecostal praise service.

Only one scar about the size of a dime remained to testify to the miracle of the unseen hand. Mother said, "That is to remind us that this really happened."

"And he [Jesus] put forth his hand, and touched him. . . ." (Luke 5:13).

This Is Amazing

Submitted by Denzil Holman

It was June 2007, gardening time in Bakersfield, California. I was working in our front yard.

As I worked, I lost my balance and tripped. I landed hard on the sidewalk. Horrible pain shot through my back. That night I awoke with fever and nausea. Later I learned that I had bruised my kidneys.

The next morning, we loaded our motor home and left for the northwest. The meetings we were to work in Oregon and Washington for the Pentecostal Publishing House waited for no man. We had many miles to travel.

As we drove through beautiful northern California, I noticed a horrible metallic taste in mouth. By that evening I had lost all taste for food. Over the next few days my legs and abdomen swelled. Each day my condition grew worse. I slept sitting up to keep from suffocating. Somehow, I managed to keep my schedule and ministered in several churches. By the time the Oregon camp meeting closed, I was in terrible condition. My legs were like sticks and horribly swollen. Phlebitis.

We left the campground and drove straight home. My wife did most of the driving, as I could only drive for about thirty minutes at a time. The rest of the time, I sat in the back seat with my legs elevated to ease the burning.

At home in Bakersfield my doctor diagnosed me with nephritic syndrome. My cholesterol was over 1300. I was in danger of blood clots. I had gained sixty-five pounds from the edema. The doctor sent me to radiology for a kidney biopsy. They asked that dreaded question, "Is there any history of cancer in your family?"

Fear tormented me.

During the nerve-wracking days of waiting for the biopsy report, we attended a special service at Pastor Dan Butler's church in Bellflower. The guest minister, who did not know me, prophesied about my fear of cancer and prayed for me.

Still waiting. Another day I felt impressed to call Harold Strange, a minister friend in Massillon, Ohio. He prayed for me over the phone and prophesied, "Your healing will be gradual, but it will begin now. The doctor will be amazed. As confirmation when we hang up, you will feel the presence of God."

We ended the call. Heaven came down. The room filled with the glory of God. For at least twenty minutes, I walked and praised God.

Still waiting, we headed to Tampa, Florida. At the United Pentecostal Church general conference, we worked for the Pentecostal Publishing House in the book area. Elder Arless Glass walked up to me and said, "I want to pray for you." Again, Heaven came down.

Back home after the conference, we returned to the kidney doctor to get the results of the biopsy. Before going into the building, I read and claimed promises from God's Word. Then I took a deep breath, and we walked into the doctor's office.

In the little the-doctor-will-be-in-soon room, more waiting. Finally, he entered. He picked up my report and started reading. A smile spread across his face. "This is better than I expected. You will not have to go on dialysis. You can write another book." Then he said the words that my friend in Ohio had prophesied, "This is amazing!"

He placed me on medication. Within two or three weeks, the sixty-five pounds of swelling were gone. After that, every time we went for a follow-up visit, the doctor would check my chart, smile, and shake his head. "This is amazing!"

"And they were all amazed, and they glorified God, and were filled with fear, saying, We have seen strange things to day" (Luke 5:26).

Three Blankets, Three Babies

Isabella Faith: God's Promise (Part 1)

As told by Tanya Gurule

Author's note. *Jacqualine, a young single lady at Christian Growth Center, Pueblo, Colorado, handed a gift to each of three childless couples. Each gift box contained a baby blanket and a letter. She told them that she had been praying for God to give each couple a miracle—a baby. Read the three parts of this story to discover the entire miracle of the three blankets.*

Tim and I were married in June of 2000. Two years later, we decided we were ready to start our family. Another three years passed. We were getting desperate. Having a baby moved from a wish to a deep desire.

In 2005 we climbed aboard the emotional roller-coaster known to many other infertile couples. Vitamins. Calendars. Wait and see.

In 2009 we endured further testing. More prodding. More exams. More waiting. The results: we were told that we would never have a child unless we adopted. Seeds of bitterness sprang up in my heart. Apparently, God's plan and my plan did not agree.

At this point, I relinquished every shred of hope that we were ever going to have a child. My lifelong dream of being a mother died. I was weary of trying, hoping, dreaming. I changed my focus. I was career bound.

No doubt, Jacqualine gave baby blankets to three wanna-be mothers to inspire faith, but I did not receive mine that way. My faith had died. No way would I ever be a mother. I did not even want to think about it.

In 2011, when Bishop John visited our church and prayed for two other childless couples, we stood back and watched. I was not going to go the route of fasting, praying, waiting any longer. God had said, "No," (I thought), so I was moving on with my life.

My husband and I had been married twelve years when again Bishop John from Africa came to minister at our church. Tim and another man from the church picked him up at the airport. In the process of transferring Bishop's suitcase to the car, it broke. Tim went shopping. When he handed Bishop John a new suitcase, he immediately prayed for Tim. He said, "A blessing you have been waiting a long time for will come to pass."

A couple of weeks later, I was suffering from flu-like symptoms, and my best friend suggested I take a pregnancy test. I did not tell Tim I was taking a test. (I did not know about Bishop John's prayer and prophecy.) When the test came back positive, I let out a shrill scream and fell to the floor in disbelief, releasing the biggest emotional tears that my body could produce.

Tim ran into the bathroom. "Tanya, are you hurt? What happened?"

Finally, I gained enough control to sob, "We are getting our miracle—our Isabella Faith."

The next day I went shopping. I bought a newborn size hot pink tutu.

My mother warned, "Tanya, you don't even know if you are going to have a boy or a girl or if the baby will survive."

"Mom, God would not make me wait thirteen years for my miracle and not give me what I want."

On April 1, 2013, our Isabella Faith sucked in her first breath and gave a vigorous cry. By the way, her name means "God's promise."

"Blessed be the Lord . . . according to all that he promised: there hath not failed one word of all his good promise" (I Kings 8:56.)

Three Blankets, Three Babies

Keelin Janae: A Beautiful Answer from God (Part 2)

As told by Kari Lee

The day after Thanksgiving 2007, I was on an operating table. Just a few weeks prior, I had sat in a cold doctor's office, listening to him calmly and clinically discuss the two large cysts that needed immediate removal. "Will I still be able to have children?" I asked.

"Well, we'll do our best...." he said, his voice trailing off. I was devastated. As a child, I dreamed of motherhood. I tenderly cared for my dolls, and, as I grew older, I always had a baby on my hip. I dreamed of the day I could cradle one of my own. Now, at the age of twenty-one, it looked like that might never happen.

Shortly before the anesthesiologist took over, I remember the doctor stopping by the table and, seeing my face, softening. "I'm going to do my very best," he promised.

Hours later, I awoke. The first words out of my mouth were questions. The nurse grabbed my hands, and, in a voice heavy with sorrow, she whispered, "I'm so sorry."

When they wheeled me to my room, I was in a ball of grief. My mom ran for anyone she could find. Soon, the nurse walked in, and I was told the most incredible story. My surgeon's wife was also a surgeon who had a practice in another state; however, she had flown down over the Thanksgiving holiday and decided to accompany her husband in the OR for the day. As my surgery progressed, it became clear that they were not going to be able to just remove the cysts. In a moment of compassion, his wife stepped in, explaining that she had learned a new surgical technique that might work. She took over the surgery—and successfully saved half of one ovary. In the flurry of all of that, my post-op nurse didn't realize what had actually happened and conveyed the incorrect news.

The next day, the doctor visited me and relayed the same story. There were a lot of unknowns ahead of me concerning my fertility, but children were not *impossible.*

A year and half later, Jeremy and I married. We didn't know what the future would look like for children, and, during the first couple of years, I had more cyst issues, which made us even more uncertain that I would be able to conceive. Years later, I would be diagnosed with PCOS, but, at the time, we just had my gut instinct that there were multiple issues complicating our ability to have children. We decided to just leave things in God's hands, and, if nothing occurred, we would pursue adoption. While I tried to be nonchalant about it, the reality was that the years of uncertainty were weighing on me. I really wanted a baby, and I was in anguish over what I suspected would be years of waiting. During this time, Bishop John Wayabire came to our church. Our pastor mentioned that he had a gift for praying for childless couples; however, I felt that was reserved for couples who had faced years and years of infertility. I was surprised when, one night, he came and prayed for me and my husband.

In the beginning of 2012, Brother Robbie Mitchell came to our church. He asked anyone who had a prayer for 2012 to come and be prayed for. My husband and I went up to be prayed for. Afterwards, another sister came to me and hugged me tightly, "God is going to give you your baby this year." The next month, another sister in our church had her newborn niece at a meeting. She asked if I wanted to hold her, and I remember feeling a wave of intense grief as I cradled the tiny baby. All night long, I felt a deep heaviness and despair.

Soon after that at the end of an evening service, Jacqualine Maurello asked if she could put a package in my car. "Open it in private," she instructed. As we sat in our car, I opened the package and pulled out a tiny blanket. "This is for the baby God is going to give you," the accompanying letter said. And I sobbed.

Not quite four weeks later, I stared at a positive pregnancy test. On November 7, 2012, after a harrowing, tumultuous pregnancy and delivery, Keelin Janae entered the world. Her name, loosely interpreted, means "A beautiful answer from God." Shortly after her birth, I was diagnosed with PCOS. Still, despite the odds, we were blessed with another daughter 4.5 years later. Together, they are a daily reminder that God sees, hears, and answers.

"I called upon the LORD in distress: the LORD answered me" (Psalm 118:5).

Three Blankets, Three Babies

Samuel: Asked of God (Part 3)

As told by Sandra Sena

Travis and I married in 2004. After three years and no baby, I started fretting. Travis assured me, "God knows when."

But for me the desire to be a mother was a soul-deep yearning, not a surface wish. Doubt plagued me daily. "You'll never have a baby." "You'll never be a mother."

Travis relented to my tears and pleas. We climbed on the wanna-be-parents roller-coaster of appointments with doctors and specialists. We endured needles, swallowed vitamins, followed schedules. We invested money, time, and energy. We clung to hope! We drained our bank account, our emotions, and our strength. We had no more to give.

The infertility road is a muddy, rutted trail, and we were barefooted. More and more I understood how the woman in the Bible with the issue of blood felt. "If I can just touch the hem of His garment." Like Hannah, my soul cried out to God for a miracle. All I wanted was to be a mother.

We started looking into adoption.

Travis and I prayed for a closer connection to God. In reply He connected us with other couples who were trudging the same rough road.

At church in 2011, a young single lady in our church brought us a gift box. In the box was a baby blanket and a letter. "I'm praying for you, for God to give you the desires of your heart." That moment faith and hope were rekindled in our souls. (Thank you, Jacqualine Maurello, for your prayers and obedience to God.)

We decided to stop all treatments, halt our adoption plans, and trust God. Our revised plan was under the care of the Great Physician. We would simply wait on God's timing. Wasn't that what Travis had been telling me all the time?

Later that same year Bishop John Wayabire from Africa held a revival at our church. One evening while I prayed at the altar, Bishop Wayabire prayed for me. The name "Samuel" reverberated in my head. God reinforced in my spirit that I was to trust him, let Him perform the miracle, and receive all the glory.

A couple months later, in the early part of 2012, we discovered that we were pregnant!

Our healthy boy was born November 2012. Guess what we named him? Samuel, of course.

Three years later we were blessed with a darling baby girl. We named her Victoria. God had heard our cry and given us victory.

"The God of Israel grant *thee* thy petition that thou hast asked of him" (I Samuel 1:17).

What a Difference

Submitted by Nichelle Lewis

Throughout my childhood, a nagging cough and shortness of breath limited my activities. When I was in middle school, a doctor prescribed an Albuterol inhaler. I didn't like it because it made me jittery. So, I did not carry it. When I had an intense asthma attack in the eighth grade, I realized that not carrying it was not the thing to do. From then on, my inhaler was my constant companion. I did not need it often, but when I needed it, I needed it.

When my husband and I moved to Kansas in 2012, my health deteriorated. In the mornings, the room seemed to spin. I had to brace myself against the walls to move from room to room. Throughout the day other symptoms ambushed me. The top of my head tingled, and I had trouble concentrating. I was exhausted and my chest felt heavy.

We were having dinner with church friends when the symptoms struck.

My friend asked, "Do you have asthma?"

I pulled out my inhaler and used it. Surprisingly, it helped somewhat. *Could I have been dealing with asthma flare-ups all the time?* Apparently so. While the inhaler gave me some relief, it did not resolve the problem. I was reluctant to go to the doctor because I assumed that he would prescribe steroids.

Service after service I asked my pastor to anoint me with oil in the name of Jesus. I did not know when or how God would heal me, but I believed He would. So, I kept asking.

We were at a Christmas banquet one Saturday evening when the asthma villain ambushed me again. I could barely breath. Exhausted I lay my head on my husband's shoulder. After the banquet I asked for prayer . . . again. Then we went home, believing God could heal me, but disappointed that He had not.

The next morning at church, the visiting minister, Tom Johnson, preached about the powerful healing virtue of Jesus Christ. I sat suffering another ambush, exhausted, struggling.

The minister declared, "The spirit of healing is present in this building at this moment." He paused, then exclaimed, "Oh!" He held out his hand as if someone had grabbed him by the wrist and led him to me. He laid his hand on my forehead and began speaking in tongues.

When he decreed, "In the name of Jesus!" something like a bolt of electricity ran from my head to the bottom of my feet. I fell on my face, praying in tongues.

It seemed only a few moments before my husband helped me to my feet. But, oh what a difference! I felt completely whole. In that stunning instant, the villain had disappeared. Every symptom had vanished. No more tingling head. No more shortness of breath. No more dizziness. Jesus had healed me!

At home I dumped every inhaler and chamber used to dispense the medication into the trash. I did not want any evidence of my affliction remaining.

Two months later when I went to the doctor for an appointment, the nurse asked me to blow into the peak flow meter. I blew.

The nurse smiled, "You are in the green."

"What does that mean?" I asked.

"It means your lungs are healthy."

Several years later, I decided to start running. Eventually, I could run for thirty minutes with no shortness of breath. Amazing! All my life I had struggled to jog ten minutes without gasping. Not anymore.

Oh, what a difference!

"Is any sick among you? let him call for the elders of the church; and let them pray over him, anointing him with oil in the name of the Lord" (James 5:14).

Miracles of Protection

God on the Battlefield

Submitted by Nathan Karriker

In the early morning of January 30, 1968, Viet Cong forces attacked thirteen cities in central South Vietnam, just as many families began their observances of the lunar new year.

"Twenty-four hours later, the PAVN [People's Army of Vietnam] and Viet Cong forces struck a number of other targets throughout South Vietnam, including cities, towns, government buildings and U.S. or ARVN [Army of the Republic of Vietnam] military bases throughout South Vietnam, in a total of more than 120 attacks.

The Tet Offensive was "an attempt to incite rebellion among the South Vietnamese population and encourage the United States to scale back its involvement in the Vietnam War."(Reference: https://www.history.com/topics/vietnam-war/tet-offensive)

Twenty-year-old E-5 Jack M. Karriker, Jr. and his buddies hunkered in their bunker while mortar fire raged around them. At least one bunker near them had taken a direct hit. They knew they were next. Fear pressed down on them. The stench of gunpowder, fire, and blood clogged their nostrils.

Jack and the other young men in the 24th Infantry, known as the "Green Lightning Bolt." were not superheroes. They were simply young men dedicated to doing what they had volunteered to do and disciplined to follow orders. At this point, it looked like the cost of their commitment would be their lives.

Back in Hutchinson, Kansas, Jack's grandmother Avery, who had recently received the Holy Ghost, and her church interceded for him.

That night in the bunker in Vietnam, the roar of war swirled in Jack's brain with the words of the Army's induction pledge:

"I, Jack M. Karriker, Jr., do solemnly swear that I will support and defend the Constitution of the United States against all enemies, foreign and domestic; that I will bear true faith and allegiance to the same; and that I will obey the orders of the President of the United States and the orders of the officers appointed over me, according to the regulations and the Uniform Code of the Military Justice. So, help me God."

Jack envisioned his lovely bride, Luanne. Their dreams of a family, a house, and a wonderful future fast forwarded through his memory bank. In desperation he fell on his knees and screamed out to the God that he had never met. "God, I do not want to die in Vietnam. Please, please, help me. If You will save me, when I get home, I will serve You."

Total silence. No voice from Heaven spoke. Only silence. Immediately the machine guns, the mortars, and the rockets stopped! Silence. The most beautiful silence Jack had ever heard.

That night Jack Karriker met God on the battlefield.

Later in another firefight, a piece of shrapnel shot straight across Jack's chest. It ripped his uniform in half. Jack felt something moist dripping near his heart. Blood? But it was not blood. It was ink! The shrapnel had hit the ink pen in his pocket. The pen had deflected the metal fragment outward. Had it gone inward or even been a fraction of an inch closer, Jack would have died instantly.

So, God brought Jack safely home. He had a place for him on another battlefield—the battlefield of spiritual warfare. Through the years, Jack kept the vow he made to God that night in the bunker in Vietnam. He dedicated his life to teaching Bible studies, winning souls, and being faithful to his God, family, and church.

How many other young men have witnessed the miraculous power of God on the battlefield? Most, like Jack, are reluctant to share their stories. Jack's prayer is that everyone who reads this account will give glory to the God of peace who intervenes on the battlefields of war.

"I will say of the LORD, *He is* my refuge and my fortress: my God; in him will I trust. Surely he shall deliver thee from the snare of the fowler, *and* from the noisome pestilence" (Psalm 91:2-3).

Oh So Close

Submitted by Dorothy Uldean Nalley

With a sigh, I settled into my recliner. My husband was bedfast, and I was his 24/7 caregiver. Every minute off my feet was a blessing.

Pop-pop-crackle-snap.

What was that? Did I leave something cooking on the stove?

I went to investigate. No. Nothing on the stove. I returned to the recliner.

Pop-pop-crackle-snap.

Again, I pushed to my feet. This time I looked out the patio door. Flames were shooting up in my neighbor's yard.

It was my worst nightmare. I panicked. I screamed, "Oh, Lord, how can I get Tom on that scooter and out of here before the fire reaches us? What if I drop him? What if. . . ?" My voice escalated as my fear intensified. Two blocks away people heard me praying. With God's help, I shifted Tom from the bed onto the scooter and guided him out of the house.

Sirens blared. A crowd gathered. Smoke curled high above the header of my house. Tears flooded my face. I continued crying for mercy as I moved Tom toward the street.

A fireman assured me, "Your house is not on fire."

"But look!" I pointed at the smoke.

He repeated, "Your house is not on fire."

I took a deep breath. The focus of my prayers changed from myself and Tom to my neighbors and the firemen.

Later I asked the fireman, "When can I go in?"

"Now. I will go with you."

Inside there was not even the smell of smoke.

The next morning my daughter and I stood in the backyard, assessing the damage. The house behind ours had burned to the ground, and the fence between our yards was beyond repair. A strip of burnt grass showed where the fire had burned oh so close—within three feet of the gas meter at the back of my house.

Across the yard my shocked neighbor was surveying his loss. "Go talk to him, Mom," my daughter said.

I picked my way across the scorched grass. "I am so sorry." My words were feeble, but what else could I say?

His words were strong and filled with awe. "I watched the fire as it headed toward your house. It was oh so close when suddenly the wind changed."

I had read many times about Jesus calming the wind. July 5, 2013, in Pasadena, Texas, the disciples' miracle became my reality.

"He caused an east wind to blow in the heaven: and by his power he brought in the south wind" (Psalm 78:26).

Praising through the Storm

Submitted by Krisann Durnford

This testimony has many participants and witnesses. The reason? It happened at the United Pentecostal Church Wisconsin junior camp, July 1997. My husband and I served on the camp administration staff.

The beautiful campground in Shawano County is surrounded by natural woodlands and working farms.

Tuesday around 3:00 PM, 250 campers between ages nine and twelve and 300 staff members were wrapping up recreation. As my husband walked toward the office, he noticed roiling thunderheads on the northern horizon racing toward the camp.

In the office everyone was busy. No one had noticed the abrupt weather change. Bursting into the office, my husband announced, "A storm is coming!"

A staff member suggested, "We have not done our practice storm drill. Let's do it before the rain starts."

As someone flicked on the weather radio, the security man announced on the camp's loudspeaker: "Attention! Staff, this is a storm drill. All campers and staff members are to report to the shelter." As heavy storms are common in the area, the staff was prepared to hurriedly move people indoors.

Little did we realize that this was more than a drill! But Jesus knew. He had nudged us to start the process. Everyone proceeded across the grounds to the large sanctuary.

I was at the front, leading a group of campers. My husband and one of the security men dashed up to me. "Quickly, but calmly, get everyone inside immediately. This is real. We need everyone sheltered within minutes." They quietly delivered the message to the adults.

Did we move without chaos? I wish. When danger arrives, human emotions escalate. But the staff did their best to protect and calm 250 frightened children. The storm hit moments after the youngsters were inside. Five minutes prior the sun had been shining.

The staff instructed the campers to huddle under the wooden pews. Teens comforted crying children. Adults crawled along the floor, touching each child's hands while thunder drowned out their words. Staff members prayed, sang worship songs, and hugged scared children. Kids prayed like they had never prayed. Several repented and received the baptism of the Holy Ghost because, as one mentioned later, "Either Jesus was coming, or we were leaving earth soon!"

The storm raged. The wind roared. Lightning flashed. Thunder rumbled. Trees crashed. Lights flickered, then went out. We were in semi-darkness. The ferocious storm lasted over an hour—a long time for children crouched under pews.

One of the camp teachers from Russia was visiting in America for the summer. This dear lady understood little English, but could she worship! She had faced danger before and knew how to handle it. Amid that crazy storm, she walked (not crawled) the aisles of that church with hands raised praising God. Her voice calmed the storm of fear inside that sanctuary. Racing hearts slowed. Tight nerves relaxed. Worship broke out under the pews.

Once the storm passed, the security personnel cautiously stepped outside. Beyond the campground and stretching across the roads were downed trees and electric lines. Sheer winds and at least two tornados had trashed the area, but miraculously the campground had not been touched! No buildings damaged. No trees down. Even the parked RVs were unscathed! God had kept His people safe.

The local authorities contacted us by radio. We assured them (and hundreds of concerned parents) that everyone was safe and accounted for. Due to the damage surrounding the campground, we were without electricity for almost forty-eight hours. Five hundred people with no water or electricity makes for an interesting week! However, months before, the Lord had prompted our camp caretaker to purchase a second, larger generator "in case we ever have a storm during camp." The staff fired up the generator for two hours of cooking and chow time. Then, they moved it to the main bathhouse and fired it up for another two hours. When the electricity came one, everyone shouted!

July 1997—the year we learned to praise God through the storm.

"For thou hast been . . . a refuge from the storm . . . when the blast of the terrible ones *is* as a storm *against* the wall" (Isaiah 25:4).

The Day I Talked to a Tornado

Submitted by Krisann Durnford

B ye! See you in a few weeks."
It was Mother's Day, 1988. I was a high school senior and had been visiting relatives in Milwaukee, Wisconsin. The sun shone brightly as I settled into my green Omni to travel back to my hometown of Beloit. I had not listened to the weather forecast and had no idea the excitement I was about to encounter.

On that warm, humid Sunday afternoon, my travel time was about one hour. My parents expected me home prior to our evening worship service. As I headed south on I-43, dark clouds gathered in the west.

Driving along the Interstate 43 between Milwaukee and the Illinois state line is like driving on top of a ridge. One can see for miles. I quickly realized an intense storm was ahead. I turned on the FM radio, but heard no weather reports. Debating whether I should pull off, I realized that the next exit was miles ahead. The wind picked up. It pulled at my small car, threatening to flip it. I saw terrified faces in a car that passed me. I was in the middle of a dangerous storm. Frantically I prayed, "Jesus, I need You right now. I have no idea what is about to happen."

Unbeknown to me, my parents at church had a distinct impression to pray for my safety. Jesus always knows what we need and when we need it. How reassuring that He has us in His hand!

I debated stopping and finding a ditch to shelter in, but there were no ditches on that ridge. The sky grew inky, greenish black—as dark as midnight. Suddenly, the wind ceased. I was driving in the calm. I knew that was not a good sign.

To the southwest the tail of a tornado formed quickly. It dipped toward the corn fields, headed my way. I (along with the other drivers on I-43) sped up. My small car shook. I pointed a finger at the tornado. "You can just stay up there, in Jesus' name!"

With my eyes on the white line, I glanced at the tornado. I sighed as its tail pulled back into the cloud. The wind churned the air as the I-43 traffic high-tailed past.

About two miles later, a torrential downpour pierced the darkness. Traffic came to a halt. While sitting on the shoulder of the road, I glanced in my rearview mirror. The darkness was behind me, but I saw the tail of that twister dancing around in the clouds as it passed over the interstate.

Soon the sun was shining. My heart was singing praises. Jesus is still the One who calms the storms. I watched Him do that for me the day I talked to a tornado.

"The LORD hath his way in the whirlwind and in the storm, and the clouds *are* the dust of his feet" (Nahum 1:3).

The Transparent Car

Submitted by Julie Carter

Our son George Elliott was two years old in 1982. We lived on a back-country dirt road in Vermont. Our house was on a slight hillside with a moderately long driveway. The rule for riding tricycles was to stay at the top of the drive in the flat section near the house.

One day our George on his tricycle strayed too near the downward sloping drive. Momentum quickly took hold. He sped out of control, out of reach. Benjamin, our eight-year-old son, stood beside me; screaming, we watched in horror. There was no possibility of running fast enough to stop little George from speeding onto the country road. To the left a car approached at a fast rate of speed. They were going to meet at the bottom of our driveway.

I prayed, "Oh, Lord, please make it fast. Don't let my little boy suffer!" I was so sure he was about to be killed.

The car and tricycle met at the bottom of the drive. The driver did not see the little boy on his tricycle. He did not even hit his brakes. Suddenly, right before my eyes, the car went totally transparent. Our little guy on his careening tricycle passed right through that car! I know. I was standing there. I saw him go through the car!

Little George Elliott continued across the road and into the ditch unhurt. About that time, the driver saw him. He slammed on his brakes and slid to a dusty stop at least five car lengths down the road. To say that we were shaken is an understatement.

Our son was a walking miracle. Or is that a riding miracle?

"With men this is impossible; but with God all things are possible" (Matthew 19:26).

Miracles of Provision

A Custom-Made Job

Submitted by Henry Buczynski

March 1988 my family moved to Ulysses, Kansas, to take a church. By church, I mean a building. My family—my wife, two daughters, and I—moved into the basement parsonage. The "church" needed repairs and TLC. A neighboring pastor from Liberal helped us get the building in shape so we could hold services.

Before we left Bakersfield, California, Pastor I. H. Terry asked me, "What are you going to do for a job to support your family?"

With the boldness of a young minister, I replied, "God will provide." God had proved Himself to us before we moved, so my faith was strong.

In Ulysses we prayed. I filled out applications. I was hired part-time to drive a bus for the Ulysses school district. The income helped but was not sufficient to provide for my family. We kept asking God, seeking Help Wanted ads, and knocking on business doors. I asked God to provide a job that would allow me to fulfill my responsibilities as a pastor, while supporting my family.

One day as I traveled to Johnson City to apply for another job driving a school bus, I passed Pioneer Electric Cooperative. I thought, *That would be a nice place to work.*

As I returned from Johnson City, I again passed that utility company.

Why don't you apply there?

I told the Lord all the reasons I couldn't work for them.

A strong impression hit me. *Go in and apply.*

I went in and checked their bulletin board. I read the qualifications for the job they had listed.

I told God, "I don't know how to do those things."

You haven't even tried. Go in and apply.

I walked into the office and filled out an application.

A few weeks and three interviews later, the company official asked, "Do you really want this job?"

I replied, "Yes, sir."

"Sit down. Let's talk." He continued, "This is a new position we have just created."

I was hired and began a long, fulfilling career.

In 2019 I told my boss, "I will be retiring next year."

He responded, "When you do, we will do away with this position."

In 2020 after thirty-one years of service, I retired with benefits from the job God had custom-made for me.

"*Oh* how great *is* thy goodness, which thou hast laid up for them that fear thee; *which* thou hast wrought for them that trust in thee before the sons of men!" (Psalm 31:19).

A Dream and a Bicycle

Submitted by Sarah Salas

Ten-year-old Sarah sighed as she watched Eddie ride his bright blue, ten-speed bicycle down the street. She wanted to ride a bicycle so much her legs ached. She knew she could do it, if only Eddie would let her try. If only she had a bicycle of her own.

She took a deep breath to strengthen her backbone and walked into the neighboring yard. "Eddie, could I please ride your bicycle . . . just a bit?"

A sly gleam lit Eddie's eyes. "You? You ride my bicycle?" He turned to his brother and scoffed, "David, did you hear that? Sarah wants to ride our bike. She doesn't even know how!"

"That's crazy," David responded. "She'll get hurt or, even worse, she'll hurt our new bike."

Sarah's lips tightened. "I don't know how. But I can learn! I'll show you I can."

"Not on our bike," Eddie said.

At the supper table that evening, Sarah poured out her frustration as she told her parents about the boys and their bike. Tears misted her mother's eyes. Her dad's heart silently wept. They were home missionaries in Hutchinson, Kansas. Money was tight. There was no extra money to buy bicycles for Sarah and her little sister, Anna.

Her dad's face reflected his heart. He tenderly said, "Sarah, tonight before you go to bed, ask God to teach you how to ride a bike."

"But how—."

"Ask God to give you a dream that will teach you how to ride a bike. Then you can tell Eddie and David that God cares about every prayer we pray. And you can show them that you can ride a bike."

Later, Sarah knelt beside her bed and prayed. She added an addendum to her usual nightly prayer. "God, please give me a dream to teach me how to ride a bike. Then tomorrow I will show those guys that I can do it!"

She climbed into bed and pulled the blanket over her shoulders. With a smile of expectation, Sarah drifted off the sleep.

She was riding Eddie's ten-speed bike. When the bike leaned to the left, she leaned to the right. When the bike leaned to the right, she leaned to the left. She kept her back straight and rode like a pro. Without one quiver of fear. Strong and confident. God was right beside her, teaching her to ride a bike!

The next morning Sarah jumped out of bed. At breakfast she excitedly related her dream to her parents. "I'm going to show Eddie and David. Today I am going to ride their bike. God taught me how."

She ran back and forth to the window, watching the neighbor's yard. The minute the boys came out to play, Sarah was out the door.

"Eddie, please, can I ride your bike today. I—"

"Sarah, I told you that you can't ride any bike, so you're sure not riding my new bike."

"But I know how now. God gave me a dream last night. He showed me how." She chattered on about how her dad told her to pray and how God answered her prayer.

The boys' mouths fell open.

"Please, guys, let me show you," she begged.

The boys looked at each other and shrugged. "Well, I guess you can try. But if you put one scratch on our bike, you'll never touch it again."

Keeping her skirt down as much as possible, she threw her leg over the bar of the bike. She pulled the pedal up on the right side, put her foot on it, and, with her heart thumping and threatening to burst, she took off down the road. For twenty minutes, Sarah rode that ten-speed as if she had been riding for years.

Her audience grew, as her parents and the boys' parents gathered on the lawn. When she finally ran out of oomph, she rode into the yard and climbed off. Laughter, hugs, and applause greeted her.

"Wow!" the boys shouted. Their eyes were big as softballs. "God really did give show you how to ride a bike."

Sarah's smile radiated joy. "He sure did. He did a miracle just for me!"

"O God, thou hast taught me from my youth: and hitherto have I declared thy wondrous works" (Psalm 71:17).

A Long-Distance Miracle

Submitted by Patricia Karlson

Friday afternoon. February 2019. Pueblo, Colorado. My phone rang. Caller ID identified it as a New York area code. I answered. It was the man who filled the propane tank at the house we had purchased while my husband was stationed at Fort Drum, New York. A few months previously, the military had transferred him to Fort Carson, Colorado. Our family had moved to Pueblo. Our house in New York was on the market. Winter in Carthage, New York, is not the best time to sell a house. My husband Matt and I were maintaining it via long distance—him from Afghanistan and me from Pueblo.

"Mrs. Karlson, I am concerned about your house. It has not used any propane all month. I think your boiler is out."

That was not what I needed to hear. The service man told me that, in the previous two weeks, the temperature in that area had dipped to -35 to -40 degrees for days at a time. At that moment they were experiencing a blizzard and already had 4-feet of snow on the ground.

Immediately, I called a plumber. His response to my plea was, "Sorry, but due to the weather, the quickest I can get there is Monday. But I really don't see any need to hurry. Whatever damage is going to be done has already been done. The pipes in your house have already frozen and burst. Nothing can be done until the thaw. When they thaw, your house will have catastrophic damage."

The house's main source of heat was radiant heat. Water pipes ran throughout the foundation and heated the house with hot water. He warned me that there would be damage not only in the walls, but also the foundation as well.

I scheduled the plumber to send someone out the first thing Monday morning.

Then I prayed.

That Sunday night my pastor preached on miracles. He said, "I feel like someone here needs a miracle tomorrow!"

Did I ever! I knelt and prayed, "God, you know I need a miracle tomorrow!"

Monday morning. My phone rang. Caller ID identified the New York area code. It was the plumber.

"Ma'am, I can't believe this, but there are no frozen pipes in your house--no damage in any way. Only a faulty thermostat that switched off the boiler. You must be the luckiest person alive!"

No, I'm not lucky at all. I simply serve the one true God who works long-distance miracles.

"Behold, I *am* the LORD, the God of all flesh: is there any thing too hard for me?" (Jeremiah 32:27).

A Memorial Prayer

Submitted by Colby Peters

Desperate times call for desperate measures. That's about where my family was in the winter of 2011. My wife, two small children, and I lived in a rural Oklahoma town about an hour's drive from Tulsa. The daily commute to and from Tulsa for work and church activities was becoming very taxing. We had recently been through some rough times on both a personal and spiritual level. To say it was time for a change of location and a fresh start would be an understatement.

As the spiritual leader of my household, I had to make a move to save everyone. The problem was that, without the green paper stuff we call money, we couldn't just leave when we wanted.

I spoke with a local realtor about selling our house. Of course, the housing market in the area was horrible, and we were set to lose a lot of money on our house. I would have been fine with getting the payoff, but that was not the case. Instead, we were set to lose thousands, and that was thousands more than we had. We were stuck.

The normal thing to do would have been to forget about moving and tough it out or get the realtor involved and take what we could get. But I believed God would help us. I had learned to trust in God earlier in life when there were no jobs in my field. God had custom crafted one for me. That gave me hope in this situation. So, we did the only thing we knew to do. Pray.

Part of the problem was that I didn't really know how to pray the kind of prayer it took to see a miracle happen. Thankfully, at about the time we started praying, a friend of mine was reading the book by Mark Batterson, *The Circle Maker: Praying Circles*

Around Your Biggest Dreams and Greatest Fears. I had not read the book nor heard about memorial prayers. I just took the concepts that the author stressed, "Bold prayers honor God and God honors bold prayers" and to "circle your problems with prayer" literally.

If God liked specific prayers, we determined that was how we were going to pray. We wanted to sell the house without a realtor with no For Sale sign in the yard. We told the Lord that we did not want to pay the closing costs. We wanted the house paid for in cash and named our price down to the dollar. Finally, we wanted this all to happen in the summer so our kids could start school at the new location at the beginning of a school year.

For the next two years . . . that's not a misprint . . . two years, I literally wore a prayer trail around our house. We had about two acres with the house in the middle. Everyone passing by could see the trail worn in the grass. We fasted. We prayed. We prayed again. We walked, prayed, circled, prayed. Were there times our faith wavered? Did we ever wonder if God was hearing us? Absolutely! But we just kept on praying.

During this time Luke 11:9 kept me walking my prayer trail. "So I tell you, keep on asking, and you will receive what you ask for. Keep on seeking, and you will find. Keep on knocking, and the door will be opened to you" (*New Living Translation*). We knew the power of daily conversations with the Almighty, so we kept asking, seeking, knocking.

Finally, one day my pastor instructed me to run a one-time ad on Craigslist about the house. He assured me that this would not conflict with my prayers. I posted it one time and never checked it nor updated it. A little over a month later, I received a call from a woman who asked if the house was still for sale. She had driven by and not seen a For Sale sign.

I still recall the evening she pulled into the driveway and the conversation that followed. Our home was an answer to her prayers. The house was everything she wanted in her forever home. Not only did she pay cash, but she bought most of the furniture, the decorations, and all the appliances.

God answered every detail on our prayer list. No realtor. No For Sale sign. No closing costs. The exact amount we ask for, and this all happened at the beginning of summer.

"And he said unto him, Thy prayers and thine alms are come up for a memorial before God" (Acts 10:4).

A Miracle in a Sack

Submitted by Charissa Smith

W e've got to sell this place and move closer to church," my husband, Shannon, said. For over a year we had driven one hour and fifteen minutes one way for every service at the Apostolic Church in Garden City, Kansas. "We're spending too much time and money on the road."

I agreed, but we lived on land my husband had inherited from his grandfather. Selling his inheritance was like digging up his roots. It was hard. We decided to put the house, shop, and three acres on the market and keep the rest of the land.

Month after month we waited. No lookers. No interest. No offers. We kept driving as we waited for our property to sell.

In the summer of 2014, I applied for and accepted a job . . . in Garden City. On July 14, I started my new job. We had mixed feelings about this—more money, but more driving.

One Sunday evening soon after, Shannon and I were overwhelmed with questions. *Is it not God's will for us to sell? Should I have accepted that job? How can we continue like this? For two years we have driven long distances to church. How long must we wait?* We laid our anxieties at the feet of Pastor Charles and his wife.

Pastor Charles said, "You must have faith. We serve a miracle-working God. Someone, a trucker or someone, will come up to your door with cash in a sack and buy your property. It will happen!"

We stared at him, raised our eyebrows, and shrugged.

His wife said, "Do you know what you just told these people?"

He smiled. "I do."

The next Wednesday I drove one hour and fifteen minutes home from work to get myself and the children ready for a revival service.

My daughter said, "Mom, don't get ready for church. Someone is coming to look at the house."

"Tonight? After months of no show, why tonight? We don't have time."

"But, Mom, he's coming."

About that time a man in a pickup drove in. "How much do you want for your property?" he asked.

I told him and asked, "But have you even looked at it?"

"No. I don't need to. How much land goes with the house and shop?"

"Three acres."

"I really need more. I have horses. Would you sell more land?"

I hesitated. "I don't know. You'll have to talk to my husband. He will be home soon. Meanwhile, I will show you around."

When Shannon arrived, he visited with the man and learned he was a trucker. They negotiated and settled on the amount of land and the price.

"I'll be back in a little bit with the down payment," the man said before he drove off.

We waited and waited. "We should have gone to church. He isn't coming back," I predicted.

Then he drove up and handed my husband a Walmart sack containing $30,000 in cash!

After he left, I called my mother who was at church. I was sobbing. She freaked out! "It's okay, Mom. We just sold our house," I blubbered. My dad, aunt, and uncle gathered around Mom as I continued, "Uncle Darwin, remember how you always say, 'If it's God will, someone will show up with money in a brown paper sack. That's how I'll know it's God's will'? Well, this trucker just showed up with cash for a down payment in a plastic Walmart sack. I guess that's good enough. We're meeting him at the bank on Saturday to close the deal."

On Saturday, the buyer met us at the bank with a suitcase filled with $120,000 in cash!

We closed that day, put an offer on a house one and one-half miles from the church on Monday, and closed that deal a few days later.

"I waited patiently for the LORD; and he inclined unto me, and heard my cry" (Psalm 40:1).

An Open Door

As told by Carol Lee

I have talked to the district superintendent. You are going for your license at the camp meeting in June." Our pastor in Minneapolis, Minnesota, told my husband David.

That was what we had been waiting to hear. For several years David had known that God had called him to evangelize. It was 1991 and God's time. We started preparing to go. We knew that soon we would be on the road . . . with no trailer, no ministerial contacts, and a blank datebook. We had three boys, an old car, and faith in the One who had called us. Excitement and apprehension swirled in our stomachs.

Soon after camp meeting and the district board's stamp of approval, our car was loaded. Loaded and overflowing with luggage in the carrier on the top of the car, stuffed in the trunk, and crammed between the two boys in the back seat. Our seven-year-old son was squashed between David and me in the front. Rambunctious boys and praying parents. We were walking (driving) through our first (and only) open door. Nebraska, here come the Lees out to save the world.

Door after door opened. The Nebraska district superintendent asked every United Pentecostal Church under his leadership to invite David to preach for them. For six months we evangelized all over the Cornhusker State.

After that David felt led to go to Wisconsin. Milwaukee, here come the Lees—wiggling boys and praying parents. A pastor we did not know asked us to preach at his church on Sunday morning. People were filled with the Holy Ghost and healed.

The pastor asked us to stay for the next two weeks and minister at his regularly scheduled services. He told David, "After that, I have already scheduled a revival with another evangelist." He told us upfront what he could pay us. It was enough to cover our hotel bill, and that was all.

No other door was open. We stayed.

We were prepared for hard times. We had a toaster and electric skillet. Eating out was not an option. I bought a whole chicken for $2.50. I fried the chicken. David recalled eating chicken and gravy over bread. The idea did not appeal to me, but I deboned the chicken and made gravy. That $2.50 chicken provided our family of five with three satisfying meals. How God stretched that chicken I do not know, but He did.

Pastors graciously allowed me to set up tables in their foyers and sell hair bows to supplement our income.

As door after door opened, David's ministry grew. Our faith stretched. Our boys grew. And our God provided. For sixteen years we evangelized.

As pastors opened their doors, God opened hearts. Blind eyes were opened physically and spiritually. Lame people were healed. Broken relationships were mended. Sinners were born again.

We never had to beg for food or a place to stay. No, we did not save the world. That was not even our job. We simply introduced people to the One who could save them, and many walked through the open door to a new life in Christ.

If God opens one door for you, don't wait for a dozen to open. Walk though that one. One is enough.

"For a great door and effectual is opened unto me" (I Corinthians 16:9).

Bread for the Eater

Submitted by Charity Kast

Money was tight at the Kasts and had been for too long. The pantry was not bare, but several shelves were empty.

One Sunday evening when the family came in from church, Dad said, "I think I'll have a bowl of cereal and a piece of toast."

Mom shook her head. "Honey, we have to save the bread for the kids' lunches."

Dad shrugged. "Then I'll have cereal."

Six-year-old Joel protested. "Mom, let Dad have toast."

"But, Joel, that bread is for sandwiches for you and Cherish."

Joel sighed. *What was wrong with Mom? Hadn't she listened?* "Mom, didn't you hear Pastor Elder?"

Mom's eyebrows crinkled. "Of course, I heard him. What does that have to do with whether or not Dad has toast?"

"Pastor Elder said, 'God gives bread to the eater,'" Joel said.

Mom grimaced. "I guess he did. Okay, Dad, I'll fix you a piece of toast."

The next day a friend's car pulled into the Kast's driveway. She unloaded loaves of day-old bread. "Look what the bakery gave me," she said. "I figured I'd share with you."

A few months later the financial situation had not changed. Money was still tight. Some pantry shelves were still bare.

Mom put aside several tea bags for the guests that she planned to invite. She was making peach tea when Joel popped into the kitchen. "Oh, Mom, are you making that gross peach tea? Please, make the good tea."

"Joel, I am saving those tea bags for guests."

Joel shook his head. "Mom, have you forgotten? God gives bread to the eater, so He can give tea to the drinker."

Mom pulled out the precious black tea bags and made "the good tea" for her family.

Fast forward to the next day. Grandmother Kast dropped by. "I was cleaning out my pantry. Don't know why I have so many boxes of tea bags. Thought I would share with you." Three boxes of 100 black tea bags.

Fast forward another day. Grandparents Buczynski came for a visit. They knew things were tight for their daughter's family, so they brought groceries. Guess what was in the top of grocery sack? Three boxes of 100 black tea bags.

Yes, Joel, God gives bread to the eater and tea to the drinker.

"For as the rain cometh down, and the snow from heaven, and returneth not thither, but watereth the earth, and maketh it bring forth and bud, that it may give seed to the sower, and bread to the eater: so shall my word be that goeth forth out of my mouth" (Isaiah 55:10-11).

God's Economy

Submitted by Deanna Barnes

A red warning light. Sizzling steam. Oil mixed with bubbling antifreeze. It happened on California State Route 120 at Tioga Pass, elevation 9,943 feet.

We had driven the car along the coasts of northern California and Oregon, toured Lassen Volcanic National Park, visited Lake Tahoe, and enjoyed side trips to ghost towns in Nevada. As we traveled toward the eastern entrance of Yosemite National Park, we caught glimpses of sparkling lakes, towering mountains, and alpine meadows dotted with purple and yellow flowers.

Instead of exploring Yosemite, however, we concluded our honeymoon trip with car trouble. All the way home to southern California, we stopped frequently as my husband tended to the overheating engine.

Days after arriving at our apartment to begin our life together, we received the expensive repair diagnosis: a cracked engine block. I had never seen my husband so upset. Fear rattled my thoughts. *Would we have enough money? What did this mean for our future?*

Money concerns often haunted my mind because I had grown up in a broken home on the fringes of poverty. Even though the Lord had always watched over my family, I had not yet developed a personal understanding of God's provision.

My heavenly Father began teaching us our first lesson in God's economy.

When my husband returned to his job, he learned that a fellow employee had a relative who worked for the company that manufactured parts for our car. Through this person, my husband bought an engine block at the wholesale price.

A representative at the car dealership taught my husband how to repair the car. A certain tool was necessary. My resourceful husband created his own version of the instrument. With help from his father, he installed the engine block and completely repaired the car.

At the end of the month, my husband walked to our apartment office to pay the rent. To his surprise, the manager said, "I'm reducing your rent this month because you were away for two weeks on your honeymoon."

The amount she deducted covered the exact amount of the car repair. In God's economy loss and gain balanced perfectly.

"The LORD will perfect *that which* concerneth me: thy mercy, O LORD, *endureth* for ever" (Psalm 138:8).

God's Investment Return

Submitted by Rick Hughes

*W*hat's that we smell? The saints sniffed. I did too. It was December in Oklahoma, and the church's heating system was spewing out threatening fumes.

I called a heating and air company. After they checked it, their conclusion was not what I wanted to hear. "There are holes in two heat exchangers. To fix them will cost approximately $10,000."

Ten thousand dollars we did not have. *Oh well,* I thought, *we'll just cripple along with it as it is until I can borrow the money or raise it.*

The heating technicians continued, "We are going to disable the units. They are too dangerous to use as they are."

So much for my idea of delaying the inevitable.

The next service was Sunday morning. The weather was tolerable. It was cool in the church, but not unbearable. But time was not on our side.

It was Christmas for Christ offering Sunday. For a minute I was conflicted. *Do we want to give to a home missions church while we sit in the cold?* The temptation passed as quickly as it came.

As I promoted Christmas for Christ and prepared to receive the offering, I said off-handedly, "If anyone has an extra $10,000, we could sure use it to fix the heating system."

Victory Worship Center was not a large church, and the people were not rich. But they were givers. That morning they gave over $2,000 to Christmas for Christ.

After the service dismissed, a man from out-of-town who had only attended our services once before approached me. "How much do you need to fix the heating system?"

I answered, "$9,500," and then sort of laughed out loud.

"I didn't bring my checkbook today. Where can I meet you tomorrow to give you a check?"

We agreed to meet for lunch, and he walked away. I fell on my knees at the altar and wept before the Lord. "Oh, God, forgive me for my unbelief."

The next day as he handed me a check for $9,500, he explained, "I haven't been going to church and am behind on paying my tithes. This will catch me up."

A small church in a small town gave what they could, and God supplied the rest.

"Give, and it shall be given unto you; good measure, pressed down, and shaken together, and running over, shall men give into your bosom. For with the same measure that ye mete withal it shall be measured to you again" (Luke 6:38).

How God Paid Our Rent

Submitted by Krisann Durnford

In May 2013 our family moved to Burlington, Wisconsin, to plant a church. For six months, my husband and I prayed through our city, met new friends, and studied the demographics of the area. We started a home Bible study and planned for our first worship service in October.

As summer ended, a tremendous spiritual battle ensued. The enemy fought and intimidated us, hoping to stop our efforts for the kingdom. Rather than give up, we dug in and claimed the ground. Several circumstances drained our finances. In October we did not have the money to pay our rent. The intense spiritual warfare disturbed our family life and sleep. Worry and fear clouded our countenances and our vision.

I re-read a wonderful book by Nona Freeman, *Bug and Nona On the Go*. My faith stirred. For several days, I prayed, "God, if You did it for them, You can do it for us."

But the struggle thickened. No matter what we did, things went askew—my husband's employer cut his work hours, our better car died, and health issues occurred. On every side more bills and less income.

In those moments I realized there cannot be a miracle without a problem. At the first of the month, I prayed, "Lord, what are we to do? You led us to this house. You called us to this city."

That weekend we visited our home church. A dear friend handed me an envelope. Our rent was paid! Thank You, Jesus!

We continued outreach and prayer. The spiritual struggle eased, but the financial struggle was ongoing. My husband applied for numerous jobs, but none were available. I was self-employed as a private music instructor. Because we had moved, my client base was small. As the weeks passed, we again prayed, "Lord, now what?"

Around mid-November a client approached me with a sizeable check. As I questioned the amount, she explained their participation in an arts program that paid for private lessons. If I would provide a receipt, they would remit payment for the entire year. I stared at the check in amazement! *These stories only happen to missionaries overseas,* I thought. Not true! They happen according to God's plan. That check paid November's rent. That same month God provided us with a ridiculously low-priced, slightly beat-up car—one my husband could use for work.

Certainly, in December things would change! No. The faith walk continued. We saved a few dollars earned from odd jobs and cashing in soda cans. Not enough for rent.

The week before Christmas my husband was driving through town. A company vehicle the next lane over swerved into his lane and broadsided him! The damage was insignificant considering how beat up the car already was, but the company contacted us immediately regarding a settlement payment. Within a week . . . our rent was paid!

For three consecutive months God paid our rent! I firmly believe it was a test of our faith and calling. We are a testimony of God's provision as we work in His kingdom. We give Him all the glory

!

"But my God shall supply all your need according to his riches in glory by Christ Jesus" (Philippians 4:19).

Miracle Biscuits

Submitted by Janet Pound

Summer 1949. Four young ladies, Marilyn Miller, Janet Smith, Alma Lee Wise, and Gracie Butler from Pentecostal Faith School in Oklahoma City headed south. Their feet were on the ground, but their heads were in the clouds, even though on their shoulders rested the responsibility of conducting a Vacation Bible School in Elmore City, Oklahoma. They were determined to do their best, trusting God to do what they could not—save souls. They were elated when the VBS exploded into a revival.

Pastor Warren Emberlin arranged for them to stay with Sister Fowler. Widow Fowler lived in a tiny three-room house with a lean-to back porch. She had one bed and a pullout couch. Each morning before the girls left to do their miscellaneous ministry duties, they gathered around the kitchen table. Sister Fowler served a hardy farm breakfast of eggs, biscuits, and gravy.

One morning Sister Fowler said, "Girls, I want to tell you something about these biscuits. They are miracle biscuits." She pointed at the old-fashioned stand-alone cabinet with the flour bin and shifter on one side. "One morning during the Depression when my kids were still at home, I went to the flour bin. There was enough flour to make one batch of biscuits. That was all."

"I prayed, 'Lord, this is it. I'm going to make biscuits for my family this morning, then that's it.' There was no money to buy more flour. The next morning, I went back to the cabinet and out of habit opened the flour bin. Lo and behold, there was enough flour to make another batch of biscuits. Since then until today, there has always been enough flour in the bin for one more batch of biscuits."

As tears rolled down the girls' faces and praises filled the kitchen, they buttered and ate their miracle biscuits.

The Great Depression was 1929-1933. The girls ate the miracle biscuits in 1949. For some sixteen or twenty years the flour bin had never been empty. No one living knows how many more years God provided flour for that little lady in Elmore City. As God provided bread for the little widow in Elijah's day, so He provided bread in the twentieth century for Widow Fowler.

"*And* the barrel of meal wasted not, neither did the cruse of oil fail, according to the word of the LORD, which he spake by Elijah" (I Kings 17:16).

Miracles Big and Small

By Mary Loudermilk

I grew up hearing my parents talk about miracles God performed in their lives. Talking about God's goodness was just part of their normal conversations. It was "God talk" at home, rather like Deuteronomy 6:7.

Recently, my niece and I spent time going through one of my dad's old scrapbooks. A newspaper clipping from the 1930s caught her eye. Pictured was a group of men in work clothes and hard hats. The article told of one worker whose life was miraculously spared when a heavy object fell on his head. The hard hat saved the man's life. That young single man was my dad. While I don't remember him telling that particular story to me, without that miracle, I would never have existed.

Dad told us the "nickel story" many times. In today's world a nickel is insignificant. I leave loose change in the console of my car without thinking about it. But in the 1930s a nickel would buy something. Dad grew up in a family that wasn't religious, but somehow, he found Truth and gave his heart to God. At that time, he still lived at home and worked in his father's country store. I had the impression my granddad didn't pay him an actual wage. Once my dad started attending church, he would take a coin from the cash drawer to give as an offering at church. Then God convicted him of taking money from the till to put in the offering. One night as he lay in bed praying about having no money to give at church, he felt something drop into his hand—a nickel. God provided the offering.

Perhaps the story I heard most often was of my father's healing from tuberculosis. No bed was available in a sanitarium, standard treatment in those pre-antibiotic days, so he was confined at home. By this time, he had met my mother, and his thoughts had turned to love and marriage. All that was on hold because of the tuberculosis. Being a serious young man, he didn't want God to think he only wanted his healing because he was in love. (I don't think God would have minded.) He promised the Lord if he were healed, he would wait six months to marry. This wasn't something God required but something he chose to prove his sincerity toward the Lord. When friends from church came to pray for him, he coughed up the infection and was instantly healed. Six months later as he and mom applied for their marriage license, the sign on the counter read, "Today is the day!" Dad had kept his promise to the Lord—to the day.

Fast forward many years, and Mom was widowed and living on Social Security and a small pension from her years working for the school system. She needed some expensive dental work. The kindhearted dentist allowed her to make monthly payments. Mom did not like debt and constantly worried about owing so much. I assured her God was taking care of the matter by the dentist allowing her to make payments. She thought God could just provide the money, so she prayed.

Shortly after this, she received a letter stating that the state legislature had reviewed the pension plan and increased the monthly pay of those making under a certain amount. Her small pension almost doubled. Mom's prayers not only gave her a miracle; they blessed many others with the same pay increase.

Not all miracles are of earth-shaking proportions. They can be as simple as a nickel in a new convert's hand or as complex as a legislative body changing a pension plan. God does some miracles behind the scenes and anonymously. Only later do we realize it was His work.

I'm so thankful my parents shared the stories of His blessings in their lives. It allowed me to understand how He takes care of us in all of life's situations. Whatever the miracle you need is big or small, God is at work in your behalf.

"Casting all your care upon him; for he careth for you" (I Peter 5:7).

One Little Wish

Submitted by Anna Ballinger

When Daniel and I first married, money was so tight pennies squeaked. He worked a job that did not have benefits, and, during the Kansas winter, little extra work was available. Making ends meet was like trying to stretch a leather belt. By the beginning of summer 2013, our finances were extremely slim due to a slow season in the welding business.

Then came watermelon season. One Thursday evening as we sat down to supper, I told Daniel, "I am really craving watermelon. It sounds delicious."

He agreed. "Man! That does sound good."

But we had no money until the next week's paycheck, and that check was already allocated. Sorry. No watermelon for us that week or the next . . . or so we thought.

Friday morning as I was cleaning house, Sharon Morey, a faithful saint in the church we attended, knocked on our door. She stood on our porch holding a watermelon.

I invited her in. She told me, "When I went to the grocery store this morning, watermelons were on sale two for the price of one. I thought, 'Oh my! A watermelon sounds delicious! But, how on earth am I going to eat two?' Then I heard that still, small voice, 'Buy one for yourself and take one to Daniel and Anna.'" She smiled. "So, here I am!"

My tears collided with my smile. In amazement, I thought, *We didn't even pray for a watermelon. We simply wished.*

I wrapped my arms around my friend and squeezed. "Last night Daniel and I talked about how good watermelon sounded, but we have no money to buy one. Thank you so much for being

sensitive to God! He truly does care about the little things."
Even one little wish.

"If ye shall ask any thing in my name, I will do *it*" (John 14:14).

One Step at a Time

Submitted by Karen Brown

Economic recession = mental depression = desperation. That described me and many others in the state of Oklahoma in the spring of 1985.

Please, God, help us out of this black hole.

He did. One step at a time. First step. My husband David and I searched the skimpy Help Wanted ads. We applied. We prayed. Days passed. No jobs, not even interviews. The cash flow stopped.

On top of our financial situation, my back was out of whack. I endeavored to deal with it without complaining (at least, with minimal complaining) while caring for our three children and home. With no money and no insurance, going to the doctor was not an option.

When I heard about a program at the local technology school where women attended school on a Displaced Homemakers grant, I took another step. I enrolled in business classes.

One Sunday morning I felt something slip in my back. I fell unconscious. As I was moving in and out of consciousness, my husband and children helped me into the living room, where I lay on the carpet. We called my pastor's wife, Barbara Westberg, who lived twenty miles away.

When she arrived, she asked, "Do you want to go to the hospital?"

"No. We don't have insurance. Take me to the church and let Brother Westberg pray for me."

Agonizing step by step with my husband and my pastor's wife assisting me, I made it to the car. By the time we arrived at church, the service was almost over . . . everyone thought. As my pastor prayed for me, a prayer meeting erupted. Unassisted,

I walked one step at a time around the sanctuary praising God, gaining strength and speed with each round. After church, I walked to the car unaided.

In the college town near where I lived, the semester was wrapping up. Everyone was looking for work. I had asked my instructor if she could find an internship for me so I could gain experience. I knew we could survive on the grant for a short while. But I had to have experience to get a permanent job.

God had touched me on Sunday, but I was still not up to par. Wednesday I called my instructor to explain why I could not be in class.

She said, "That's fine. As soon as you get back, I have an internship for you at a local doctor's office."

By Monday I was on the job! That internship turned into a full-time paid position.

My financial and physical healing did not happen instantaneously. One step at a time God led David and I out of depression and desperation. In Oklahoma, the recession continued for some months, but with God's help we were back on our feet and moving forward. Thirty-four years later, I have never again had back problems or been without a job.

"Cause me to know the way wherein I should walk; for I lift up my soul unto thee" (Psalm 143:8).

The Cotton-Candy Coat

Submitted by Anna Ballinger

When I was 12, we went to Colorado Springs to visit our family for Christmas. While we were there, we went shopping at the mall.

While rummaging through a rack of coats, I fell in love. I ran my fingers through the soft luxurious pile of a pink fur coat and pressed my face into it. "Mom! Sarah! Look at this coat! It looks like cotton candy. And it's my size, too."

"How much is it?" Mother asked.

I knew she would. Reluctantly, I showed her the tag. $129.00. I had a reputation for gravitating to the highest priced item on the rack.

Mother opted for her cop-out reply. "You'll have to ask your dad."

At the car I described the gorgeous coat with all the adjectives my 12-year-old brain could recall. Of course, Dad asked the inevitable question. "How much?"

I mumbled the figure.

His eyebrows shot up. "One hundred twenty-nine dollars! That's a lot of money." He resorted to his funny-guy tactic. "I'll tell you what, Sissy. We are coming back in a couple of months. If that coat is still there and on sale for $19.99, I'll buy it for you." He chuckled. *Good luck with that one.*

I replied with the standard family response to the impossible, "Okay. I'll pray about it." And I did, until life pushed my request to the back of my mind.

Two months later we were back in Colorado Springs at the same mall. One department store had a big sign plastered on the window: "Going out of business." Everything was greatly discounted. Because of the cluttered merchandise, I did not recognize it as The Store . . . until I rummaged through a cluttered rack. There it was . . . The Cotton Candy Coat.

My memory went into overdrive. Light flashed. I grabbed the coat and ran to find my mother.

"Mom! Mom, look! I found it. This is my cotton candy coat! It's on sale. Can I get it?"

Then came the inevitable question. "How much?"

Holding my breath, I dug for the tag. Guess what? $19.99. I jumped for joy.

Mom laughed. "Who would have thought? $19.99! Your dad promised. You prayed. It's yours."

At the car, I pulled the cotton candy coat from the sack and rubbed Dad's whiskers with the furry coat. He chuckled. "Anna, only you could get God's attention about a pink fur coat."

My dad was seldom wrong about anything, but he was wrong that time. Any 12-year-old can get God's attention if they tell Him their heart's desire.

"Delight thyself also in the LORD; and he shall give thee the desires of thine heart" (Psalm 37:4).

The Makings of a Miracle

Submitted by Denzil Holman

W e were in an extensive remodeling program in the church in Norfolk, Virginia, where I pastored. In order to put more money into the building fund, I worked part time as a piano tuner and salesman to cover the expenses of our family of five.

My three children pled, "Dad, would you buy us bicycles? Please. All the kids the neighborhood have bicycles . . . all but us."

How I wanted to, but we had no extra funds. "I will as soon as I have enough money," I promised.

When my son told a neighbor boy about my promise, the kid heckled him. "Yeah! I bet."

Not being able to give my children what they wanted distressed me. *Every kid needs a bicycle*, I thought.

Every Thursday evening the *Tidewater Trading Post* filled with classified ads comes out. I picked up one at the convenience store and flipped through it. An ad caught my eye.

For sale: Vintage Steinway piano $400.00.

I did not have $400.00, but I called anyway and arranged to go see it early the next morning. When I walked into the house, I saw the piano in terrible condition with stacks of yellowed sheet music on the top. But the metal plate "Steinway and Sons" told me that I had found a treasure. I borrowed the money and purchased it.

We moved it into our garage. My wife, three children, and I made restoring it a family project. When the piano was refinished, it was stunning! I advertised in the *Tidewater Trading Post:*

For sale: Vintage Steinway piano. $4,400.00.

A nurse and doctor came to look at it. The doctor told the nurse, "If you don't buy it, I will." Sold.

With the money, we climbed out of our financial shortage and purchased three bicycles.

Sometimes God hands us the makings of a miracle and says, "Here is what you need. Work with Me."

"For we are labourers together with God" (I Corinthians 3:9).

The Miracle of the Blue-Goose Peas

By P. D. Buford

In the 1860s–1870s Great Uncle Newton Cooper rode the Chisholm Trail from San Antonio, Texas, up to Abilene, Kansas. Newton died in the 1930s but had a son, Little Newt, who also was an outdoorsman, cowboy, and rancher in southwest Louisiana.

Uncle Newt (Little Newt) and his wife, Aunt Mittie (my mother's half-sister), were God-fearing, praying people. In the earlier part of the twentieth century, when times were hard and money tight, with many mouths to feed, Uncle Newt decided to go hunting, trusting God to help him put food on his table. It was coming up on Thanksgiving, and Uncle Newt wanted some meat for the holiday dinner. Early one foggy morning, he prayed that God would provide meat to feed his family. With the fog so thick he couldn't see the trees, he started walking to the woods behind the house. He heard geese honking as they flew over in the dense fog. He aimed his old shotgun in the air and pulled the trigger, not seeing any geese at all. In a few seconds he heard a loud commotion as something hit the tin roof of the barn. He ran to the barn, and miraculously, Uncle Newt had shot and killed a blue goose.

When he got the goose home and began dressing it, he discovered dried peas in its "crop" (usually known as the "craw," a sac-like enlargement of a bird's gullet). Uncle Newt saved the peas and cooked the goose for the family.

The dried peas were planted the following spring. Ever since then, the following generations have planted, harvested, prepared, and eaten the "blue-goose peas." With thanksgiving, the family members have always set aside some of the peas to plant the next year. The peas have been handed down from generation to generation, now for five generations and counting.

Uncle Newt and Aunt Mittie Cooper, God-fearing, praying people, acknowledged God's provision in His sending a blue goose along at just the right time and allowing Uncle Newt to kill the goose at the crucial time when the family desperately needed food. The "blue-goose peas" are now an ongoing family heirloom, treasured as a tribute to Jehovah-Jireh—the Lord will provide!

We have some of those blue-goose peas today.

"How great are his signs! And how mighty *are* his wonders! . . . his dominion *is* from generation to generation" (Daniel 4:3).

The Missionary and the Hen

Related by Marilyn Chennault

Katherine Hendryx was a Pentecostal missionary in China during a civil war. Soldiers put her under house arrest. Day and night, guards stood at her door. She had only the food the guards gave her, and that was not much.

One day while in conversation with God, she said, "I am so hungry for an egg."

The next morning, she heard scratching at her kitchen window. She went to check. A hen was sitting on the window ledge. "Cluck-cluck-cluckcluckcluck." The hen flapped her wings and flew to the ground. The American missionary, God's friend, smiled. In her window lay a fresh egg.

"Thank You, Jesus!" she sang. That morning she had a fresh egg for breakfast.

The next morning, the hen was back. "Cluck-cluck-cluckcluckcluck."

Another fresh egg for the hungry missionary's breakfast.

Morning after morning, the hen laid an egg in the window.

What about the guards? They never caught on. Chickens were everywhere. A chicken in the window? No big deal.

Until Sister Katherine Hendryx was released, she had a fresh egg for breakfast every morning.

Sometimes God takes care of us in supernatural ways, like a hen in a window or replenishing the meal and oil. At other times He takes care of us in ordinary ways that we may easily overlook.

Watch for your miracle. It could be as close as your kitchen window.

"Or if [s]he shall ask an egg, will he offer him a scorpion? If ye then, being evil, know how to give good gifts unto your children: how much more shall your heavenly Father give the Holy Spirit [or a fresh egg] to them that ask him" (Luke 11:12-13, brackets the author's).

The One-Day Answer

By Susan Bickford

S ometimes the answers to our prayers arrive after many years, and sometimes they come the same day. This was the case for me in the late 1980's, when I was much younger, both physically and spiritually. I possessed an untried, childlike faith, and had recently heard a sermon about being specific with our prayers.

Every day I was driving an old car with a broken speedometer to work. As a result, I had received a speeding ticket.

My husband and I had not yet discussed buying another car. But it seemed that this morning as I knelt in prayer, God said, "Try Me!"

I replied, "God, I really could use a car with a working speedometer." I didn't belabor the point, but went on with my prayer, praising God for His goodness. I got up and went about my day.

That evening my husband said, "I was getting a haircut after work, and the barber said he had a car that we need to buy."

Imagine my surprise and excitement! *Wow, God, that was fast!* I thought.

We went immediately to the barber's house to look at the car. It was a beautiful blue Oldsmobile that had been garage kept and had low mileage. It was the nicest car I had ever even dreamed about owning. The owner was asking an extremely reasonable price. He said, "Take it for a test drive, and pray about it. You can let me know later what you think."

I thought, *No need to pray about it. I already have!* That car gave us many years of trouble-free service and will always stand in my memory as the one-day answer to my prayer from an ever-faithful God.

By the way, the speedometer worked perfectly.

"Incline thine ear unto me: in the day when I call answer me speedily" (Psalm 102:2).

Twice Tripled

Submitted by Rick Hughes

My wife and I sat in the den of the home of our pastor and district superintendent, R. D. Whalen. "We feel like we should be doing more for God."

After listening to us ramble on, giving him suggestions as to how we could be more involved in the local church, he nodded, "You kids are going to Ponca City."

We were speechless! Ponca City was a nice town, but moving was not on our agenda. I had a great job. We were young marrieds, loved the Oklahoma City church, and were content to stay there.

He continued, "You are going this weekend to check out the city and pray. You will let me know your answer next Monday." So, we checked out the city and prayed, and on Monday answered, "Yes. We will go."

"Good," he answered. "You'll start on Wednesday. They will be expecting you."

We went. *They* were two men—the entire congregation. The building needed major repair. A stack of unpaid bills lay on the pastor's desk. We moved. God blessed. The congregation grew. We repaired the building, and, with help from our UPCI section, the bills were paid.

Ten years later, our church was landlocked and needed to relocate. An office complex north of town was for sale. It was three times the size of our present building. The owner, an attorney, said, "If a church buys this building, I will rebate them $40,000 at closing."

I doubted that, but we negotiated and arrived at a price we could manage. At closing, the attorney wrote us a $40,000 check. He came to our opening service and became our friend.

By 2006 we needed to move again. We had plans drawn for a new building but felt checked by the Spirit.

The church board president said, "Pastor, we need Central Baptist Church. It's in a great location, large enough for us, and it is for sale."

I shook my head. "I don't like that building. It's ugly."

Later I saw a realtor's flier and noticed that the price had been lowered. On a whim I called the board president. "Do you and your wife want to go with us to look at Central Baptist Church?"

Of course, they did.

The location was right. The size was right, three times our present building. The price was still out of our congregation's reach.

On the parking lot our realtor asked, "Rick, how much do you want for your current building?"

I laughed. "We haven't even thought about it. We're simply looking at this building on a whim."

She replied, "I might have a buyer for you. She will be there tomorrow afternoon to look at it."

The next day a lady representing the realtor's church toured our building. Within six weeks our old building was sold for our asking price, having never been officially on the market.

We negotiated on the Central Baptist Church facility and purchased it. We had enough money to make a good down payment with money left for renovation. After that move, the congregation again grew tremendously.

Twice God tripled the size of our church facility. From the day Pastor Whalen said, "You kids are going to Ponca City," until this writing, God has marvelously twice tripled the size the church facility in Ponca City, Oklahoma.

"Enlarge the place of thy tent, and let them stretch forth the curtain of thine habitations: spare not, lengthen thy cords, and strengthen thy stakes" (Isaiah 54:2).

Made in the USA
Columbia, SC
20 August 2024

40823222R00109

Made in the USA
Columbia, SC
03 March 2025

54662259R00087